About the Author

Nicholas Finnegan sunk down to a really low point in his life and eventually reached a stage of considering suicide. Upon reaching this point, he realized that life itself is the most important thing in the world to him and now cherishes it more than anything.

He has overcome massive emotional struggles and has changed his own life for the better and is now set out to share the amazing discoveries learnt to benefit all of our lives.

Nicholas has a deep love and passion for 'life' overall and is constantly sharing new discoveries to benefit us in as many different areas of life as possible. He has dedicated his own life to make our lives a continuous growing experience in the areas we most need to improve in.

If Nicholas is not learning something new to improve our lives, he is putting in time and energy to experience something new for the positive benefits of others.

Nicholas is always aiming to learn more to give more back and is a dedicated life time learner in understanding how to create what is needed within us to succeed.

He makes his rest place in London England, contemplating on the future of humankind; and studying martial arts and human development like a mad man!

Order this book online at www.trafford.com/06-3229
or email orders@trafford.com

Most Trafford titles are also available at major online book retailers.

Note for Librarians: A cataloguing record for this book is available from Library and Archives Canada at www.collectionscanada.ca/amicus/index-e.html

ISBN: 978-1-4251-1470-1

We at Trafford believe that it is the responsibility of us all, as both individuals and corporations, to make choices that are environmentally and socially sound. You, in turn, are supporting this responsible conduct each time you purchase a Trafford book, or make use of our publishing services. To find out how you are helping, please visit www.trafford.com/responsiblepublishing.html

Our mission is to efficiently provide the world's finest, most comprehensive book publishing service, enabling every author to experience success. To find out how to publish your book, your way, and have it available worldwide, visit us online at www.trafford.com/10510

www.trafford.com

North America & international
toll-free: 1 888 232 4444 (USA & Canada)
phone: 250 383 6864 ♦ fax: 250 383 6804 ♦ email: info@trafford.com

The United Kingdom & Europe
phone: +44 (0)1865 722 113 ♦ local rate: 0845 230 9601
facsimile: +44 (0)1865 722 868 ♦ email: info.uk@trafford.com

10 9 8 7 6 5 4 3

HIGHER SELF ESTEEM AND MORE...

Growing to Become More of where You Currently Are in Your Life

Nicholas Finnegan

Email the Author

The author always appreciates hearing from you and learning about how much you enjoyed this book and how it has helped you.

If you wish to contact the author or would like some more information about this book, please do not hesitate to email Nicholas Finnegan at:

Theborne@hotmail.co.uk

Dedication

This Book is dedicated to every human on the earth that possesses the wonderful gift of LIFE!

Introduction

The boy lives a happy life, filled with laughter and joy. He is 17 years old and enjoys going to school. He is not particularly clever and finds his lessons long and boring. He cannot wait for lunch times to arrive, so he can enjoy the company of his friends. He lives in the moment and everything is the way how it should be, fun, joyous and playful as each day goes by. Months pass as feelings begin to change. People act differently around him. Two faced friends that now speak behind his back. A lack of love received from others and a lacking of love for himself. A growing addiction to cannabis and alcohol as this seems to be the only way to cope with his problems. As time goes by his life becomes bitter. There is a loss of hope for this once joyous boy. His life is now filled with loneliness, sadness, a lacking of self love and deep regret. Is there any hope left in this world? Why is he alive? What is the reason for being here? Months and months of loneliness go by as he feels worse day by day. Should he take his own life? Is he willing to live the rest of his life feeling this way? NO! He is not! He Screams at the top of his lungs, picks himself up and begins searching for answers. The boy finally learns "We only have one life and plenty of time to live each day to its maximum potential". The boy reads and studies obsessively, book after book and new experience after new experience. He learns and widens his possibility outlook. Surely, new feelings grow to become more than he has imagined possible. He obtains a wonderful new hunger for knowledge and a new meaning for living. A year passes and this once "low self esteemed boy" is now filled with more joy than ever before. New friends are now made easily, once hard challenges are now far more enjoyable and as these new emotions grow, he will never forget what had happened to him and what he has learned due to an unpleasant experience, long time ago.

- Anything is possible when we put ours mind to it.

The boy in this story is me, Nicholas Finnegan.

I have taken the time to write this book for those particular people that may be feeling a lack of self esteem and/or self confidence. This book is also for those who are pretty comfortable with themselves and their lives right now, but really desire more and don't know how to unlock their true potential. This is also for the person that is already successful, and wanting to use their success with more precision.

Since I was a victim of low self esteem, a lacking of confidence, paranoia and a major fear of interacting with people, I knew I had to start looking for answers. I was not willing to give up on myself and in you making the decision to pick up this book, demonstrates that you are willing to do what it takes to grow and become more within your life.

In this book you will learn:

- How to become more self reliant
- Learn how to take conscious control
- To demolish negative thinking and feelings into dust
- Gain powerful self esteem and confidence within yourself
- How to handle people and negative situations
- Gain a trustful friendship within yourself that allows you to grow as a human being - in a positive and fulfilling way
- Give you the tools to succeed throughout your everyday life

During my period of low self esteem, lacking of confidence and paranoia, I deeply thought to myself "what went wrong?" "Why do I feel this way?" When I really began to think about it I realized I wasn't always lacking in self esteem. I was once a bright and happy person, so I began searching for answers.

During this book we will be learning and understanding many of the discoveries I have personally encountered over the years in helping me to develop my very own self esteem. We will also be focusing on developing your very own self esteem and confidence, so you will begin to feel better within yourself today.

We are not born with low self esteem or a lacking of confidence. We only accidentally learned non-beneficial habits of thinking and behaving that were likely to be taught by parents, teachers and/or peers. Low self esteem, a lacking of confidence, depression, paranoia and so on…are not diseases. They are just habits of thinking, feeling and behaving that we pick up over a particular period of time, usually during childhood.

The problem is we are usually not aware of when the learning phase is taking place. And when we do become aware it's already too late, as the feelings that we have learnt already become our daily habits.

We have become so good at doing this that we learn all sorts of different unpleasant habits on a consistent basis, even when we ultimately do not want to. In short, any of the negative experiences you maybe feeling right now that are holding you back, are just learned habits that we plan to change into new positive ones that serve you during this book.

This book is aimed to achieve the following self discoveries:

- How to understand and regain control of your emotions and your life
- De-programme those low self esteem habits you have
- What self esteem and confidence really is...
- How to gain higher self esteem...?
- Learning these higher self esteem habits
- And using higher self esteem to succeed in your life!

You are not alone in this book. I will not just give you information and let you get on with it. Rather I have structured this entire book so we can follow along together as you do the exercises!

Think of this book as a course in you achieving the level of higher self esteem, confidence and the value of life you truly deserve. When you think about it in this way, you will find this book to be far more enjoyable and rewarding.

Acknowledgements

I'd like to thank my family, especially my mother for helping me to understand life from different points of view.

Thanks to Nadime and Jordan Gauzee who opened my eyes to the life, discipline and respect of martial arts.

I want to thank everyone that has treated me ignorantly as if I meant nothing, if it weren't for you people this book wouldn't exist.

Also, a special thanks to everyone that has supported me in their own unique way. If it weren't for you guys I'd probably be dead! And now on with the show...!

Contents

Part One
Higher Self Esteem

Part Two
Taking Control

Part Three
Deprogramming Negative Patterns and Habits

Part Four
Using Positive Patterns and Habits Effectively

Part Five
Handling People and Your External Reality

Part Six
The Time Has Come

PART ONE

HIGHER SELF ESTEEM

The Difference between Self Esteem and Confidence

Some people can get self esteem and confidence muddled up. When I look back to what I first considered confidence to be, I imagined an outspoken person that didn't care what other people thought - and so; they did whatever they pleased.

This is simply not confidence and displays arrogance and selfishness. Self esteem and confidence are very different and having only one of these qualities, can help us in gaining the other. Gaining higher self esteem allows us to handle situations more confidently, just as self confidence contributes to our growing self esteem.

Let's now separate the two so we can understand them more clearly. After all if we are going to effectively gain higher self esteem and confidence, we must know what we are actually trying to strengthen within ourselves to achieve this.

Confidence

There are two aspects of confidence.

The First

Confidence implies facing your fears. We all have barriers in our lives that we would like to overcome.

For example: How do you feel about public speaking? Do you think you can do it? Would you do it if you were asked?

Some people that have never stood in front of a large audience and presented a speech before, may feel slightly uncomfortable about the very thought of public speaking. This is mainly because they are not used to it. If you have never publicly spoken before, how would you know what to expect from yourself or the audience?

Usually people that lack confidence think of the worst possible outcomes before they even step into these new situations. "What if they boo me, point and laugh, throw things at me and tell me to get off the stage?" No wonder why it can seem difficult to face our fears. The very thought of public speaking now seems like a crazy thing to do. Especially if something embarrassing or painful were to happen.

Fear of the unfamiliar keeps these particular people stuck. They want to take on these new experiences they desire and would very much like to have

confidence. But they think of the worst possible outcomes before they even take one step forward.
Almost as if they are faced with the decision whether or not to put their hand into a flame, with the potential risk of being burnt.
They focus on the potential risk, rather than the benefits of their outcomes.

A casual friend of mine decided he wanted to do something outrageous and exciting, so he enrolled for a sky diving lesson. Once in the air strapped to the instructor, ready to take that giant leap of death, he became shook up and couldn't get himself to do it. However after some reassurance from his instructor, he finally went through with it and experienced one of the most thrilling episodes in his life to date. And he now looks forward to doing it again and again.

When you find that you have become used to doing something despite its risks; it becomes something you have already done, therefore it is not a big deal anymore.

Can you notice the pattern here?

GAINING MORE CONFIDENCE REQUIRES YOU TO OVERCOME A FEAR OF DOING SOMETHING!

You must expect things to not go perfectly smooth all the time and realize **it's just a learning experience.** What doesn't kill you only makes you grow stronger!

When you keep practicing in something that's new to you - you usually 'stink' at first, but gradually you get better at it don't you? This principle is the same in gaining confidence in **every area of life.**

You must **accept** that the worst COULD happen. And with practice you will find yourself getting better and better at achieving what you want.

Do not practice being afraid of the unfamiliar, otherwise you will get good at being afraid of it. Instead **accept** that things will not go absolutely perfect the first time round, and you will begin to experience a **willing-ness** to reach the level of confidence you deserve.

People that have obtained confidence now just go for it, and do not allow their fear to hold them back from achieving what they want.

If you were to think about unfamiliar situations in this way, doesn't it feel necessary to accept the initial struggle at first, so you can experience more wonderful feelings further down the road?

The second

Having the confidence and tenacity to go after what you deserve in life, without worrying what "might" happen if it doesn't work or if a temporary problem gets in your way. This allows you to be comfortable within your own skin.

Life is at times about letting go and having fun in the moment. And by coming out of your shell and expressing your personality's full potential to create what you want in life. You are displaying a natural confidence within yourself to succeed in whatever you choose.

This is the new attitude towards gaining confidence we must use and embody within our being; To endure and stand up to those 'what it seems to be inflexible' barriers that used to get in our way.

Self Esteem

Self esteem is the **value** you place upon yourself.

When we have high self esteem we are in a sense our own best friends. We praise ourselves, notice our positive qualities, encourage ourselves and experience a deep rooted self assurance and value for who we are as people.

A person that has somewhat low self esteem - is the complete opposite of this.

Jane and Barbara were slightly out of shape so they decided to hire a personal trainer together. The personal trainer's main goal was to push these two women really hard so they could get the most out of their training sessions together. The exercise drills were extremely difficult for Jane and Barbara. So much so that their bodies drew close to failure on the first day of training.

On the second day of training Jane and Barbara were pushed hard once again. Barbara whined and complained saying "I can't do it anymore, I quit!" and gradually gave up on herself. Jane continued to push herself as she believes that she deserves to be in better shape and feel great!

A month later of training (and Barbara's constant whining) Jane significantly improves in her overall fitness level. Barbara did not achieve as much of a result as Jane - but still achieved enough to be grateful for.

Jane felt great about her achievements, while Barbara put herself down for not trying as hard as she could have.

Although both women achieved a significant improvement in overall fitness, Barbara failed to recognize her talents due to the doubting of her own ability. This only made her regret the entire experience instead of being proud of her accomplishments. Jane's higher self esteem allowed her to appreciate a life changing experience. And she now motivates herself to keep pushing to gain new levels of fitness.

This example shows us the effects high and low self esteem can have on our self value and capability. When you are nurturing your positive qualities, picking yourself up when troubled and encouraging yourself to do better; to be a true friend to yourself that's always praising and motivating, everything begins to fall into place.

Self esteem is about being your own best friend and noticing your accomplishments and good qualities, so you can begin to naturally feel comfortable within yourself to achieve it.

The effects on our self esteem are vast depending in which directions we head in. Low self esteem can end a person's life; where as high self esteem can make you feel on top of the world, in a way you have never experienced before.

People can generally deal with a lacking of confidence as they can deal with staying away from fear.

People can find it very difficult to deal with low self esteem. Your self esteem is ultimately the value you place upon yourself and what you believe you are capable of.

How you feel about your overall self image is basically how you feel and view yourself as a person. This ultimately determines your life experience since the way how you view and feel about yourself on a daily basis - IS YOUR LIFE EXPERIENCE!

When you begin to recognize your positive qualities, as you praise yourself for your accomplishments you will begin to feel better about yourself as each day goes by. You will find your self esteem growing each and every day as you're becoming stronger in those areas that matter to you most.

Can you imagine how good you are going to be feeling when higher self esteem is yours to own in the near future?

In a nutshell

1. Confidence is being able to face your fears; so you can overcome them and grow to become stronger in those areas that used to stop you

2. Self confidence is comfortably expressing your personality's full potential, to manifest in whatever it is you want to make new within your life today

3. Self esteem effects how you feel about yourself, your capabilities and your overall life experience

4. Self esteem is the worth and value that you place upon yourself

Self Esteem Opens the Door to Confidence

Developing your self esteem to the point where you are feeling self assured and strong within yourself is also an excellent way into gaining that level of confidence you have been yearning for.

When we achieve higher self esteem for ourselves our thinking and behaviours work with one another; this results in your **behaviours** serving your **thinking** and your **thinking** serving your **behaviours.** This allows you to make better decisions and then take action more effectively.

We stop and think about all the beneficial reasons for why we should take this action; rather than feeling stuck by thinking in terms of what prevents us from following through.

Since your mind and body are working together for you to create a more fulfilling life, you can begin to feel that trust growing within yourself. Trusting in yourself makes you **face your fear without** any fear whatsoever.

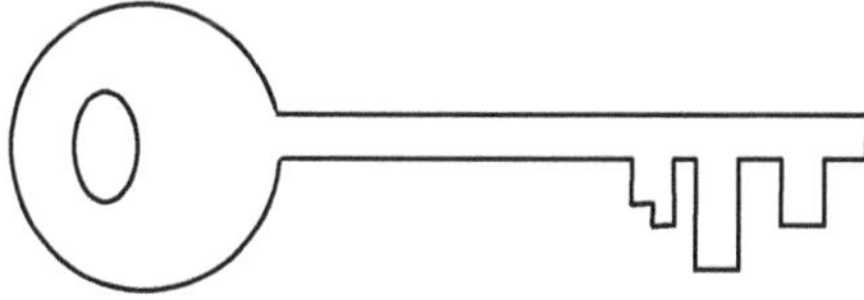

This key represents the higher self esteem that you have now achieved through using the techniques in this book. Your unconscious thinking and actions are now working in harmony together. You can now radiate a positive energy throughout your life far more easily - praising yourself for the new fulfilling emotions you are experiencing along the way.

When you achieve that level of higher self esteem, you in a sense obtain the correct key to open the door to confidence. Your new key represents that you are now working with your wants and desires - and pursuing them with inner self **assurance.**

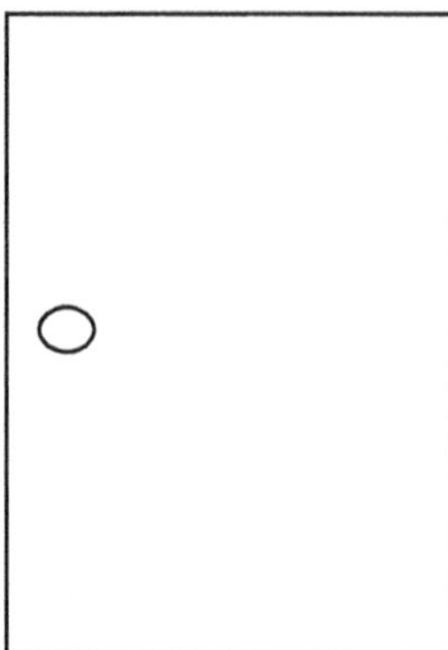

This door represent confidence, the ability to face your fears by stepping into those once weary situations and gaining that level of comfort you feel is right for you. Imagine if once you walked through this door, situations that were fearful in the past are now so easily stepped into, that you wondered what the big deal was in the first place.

Taking little risks now will not seem like a big deal anymore. As you are always naturally encouraging yourself to move forward with your higher self esteem - in a positive direction that makes you feel good about taking action.

If when we don't have any self esteem or confidence, we wouldn't likely get anywhere at all. We wouldn't possess the self esteem key to open the door to confidence and so we wouldn't be able to get in.

What happens to the majority of people that do not posses higher self esteem, is they stare at the door to confidence like a lost puppy scratching the surface wishing it would open. To put it simply there's no higher self esteem key to open the door, so they remain stuck and drool at the opportunities in life like a hungry dog waiting for Scooby snacks.

When you are working with your thoughts, behaviours and higher self esteem; you begin to approach your fears with a positive energy that allows you to always learn something new and empowering - serving you for the next time round. You will always learn something whether you have achieved your outcomes or not. This is what we are setting out to achieve - comfort, happiness and trust with your emotions. You will find yourself facing your fears effortlessly and in harmony to learn from your experiences. When you are open to your new learning's whether good or bad, the more confident you will become within your capability to take action again and again.

Our aim is to achieve high powered self esteem to open that gateway into confidence. A gateway that is always open for you to freely walk into - to experience that calm inner peaceful confidence that you desire.

If you would like, you can step into uncomfortable situations in your life right now. Forget about all the things that **could** happen and focus on the things you **will gain** as a result of taking action. As long as you are calm and congruent with your approach to seek out new learning's that serve you during your new experiences, you will do just fine!

Just make sure you always learn something that will enable you to grow even more for the future, whether your actions work out or not.

In a nutshell

1. Acquiring higher self esteem, allows you to obtain the correct key into opening that personal gateway into confidence.

2. Our aim is for your thinking and behaviours to be working in harmony together; to move forward far more easily into those desired situations

3. You will learn how to feel good about taking action. And learn from what comes from taking action, in a way that benefits you, whether you achieve your goals or not

What is High and Low Self Esteem?

We have established that self esteem represents the **value** that you have currently placed upon yourself, the value meaning your own growing self worth that you find yourself experiencing right now.

These are the three levels of self esteem:

People that experience a lower self worth

These people tend to doubt themselves or put themselves down about their capability and self image.

A neutral ground of self worth

This is something of a balance between feeling good and feeling not so good. Settling for less than you deserve as opposed to having what you really desire.

An ongoing self worth

That you are beginning to experience that grows stronger within - as you continue to recognize all your positive qualities. You will begin to improve on those particular weaknesses that you may have and consistently become stronger than you were before.

The raising self esteem metre

This diagram represents self esteem in the neutral position.

When we are in neutral, our self esteem is not so great - but not so bad either. We experience a balance of negative and positive emotions alike. Some things can be stressful and other moments can be very uplifting.

These types of people usually just 'go with the flow' and pretty much accept every moment as it comes; But really desire greater emotions and achievements out of life, as opposed to what they were currently settling for.

Higher self esteem

Gaining a higher level of self esteem for yourself will allow you to experience a deep inner connection with your emotions. You will feel this as you are living your everyday life.

Your *raising self esteem metre* will begin to look like this:

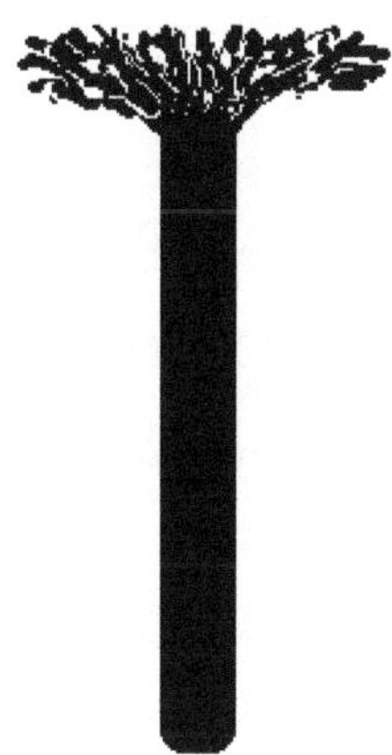

Your self esteem is now shooting out of the *raising self esteem metre* and you soon enough, find yourself feeling better day by day.

When you experience higher self esteem, you begin to feel centred and strengthened within yourself. Almost as if a safe has locked these positive feelings inside; stuck there like an iron shield protecting you from within.

These days' we hardly pay attention to who we **really** are. Life just seems to take us away into a world that is focused on our external environment.

We forget about our inner emotions of how we really feel about ourselves and our overall lives as people.

Life seems to be moving so fast; technology is always being upgraded, cars are going by, things need to be handled, bills need to be paid and you need to feed your children and yourself to live!

So many things are going on - but when you stop for a moment and find that special place inside of you that's longing to be fulfilled; it's saying to you "what about me?"

This place inside of you - needs to be nurtured by you. When we are born, we all have a major responsibility. YOU HAVE THE RESPONSIBILITY TO CONDITION YOURSELF, otherwise the world will condition you **for you**; and without asking for your permission either!!

When you do begin to nurture this place inside that needs you, it will lead into a wonderful new adventure concerning your self discovery.

Imagine if you began to discover many new empowering qualities about yourself that you weren't even aware of up until now. Can you feel how good it feels to own these feelings as your very own?

This is simply what higher self esteem is: The positive value and self worth that you are now beginning to place upon yourself.

What is low self esteem you ask?

Low self esteem - was just the opposite to higher self esteem.

In a nutshell

1. When you have higher self esteem you encourage, appreciate, praise and respect yourself

2. Higher self esteem will be focusing on everything that allows you to become happier, stronger and growing to feel more positive about yourself

People with low self esteem do the opposite to the above!

So, if you're putting yourself down or attacking your self worth in any way that prevents you from gaining the feelings you truly desire. STOP IT NOW!

The Two Worlds

External world

The external world highly affects a persons' self esteem. Many people tend to focus on the outside world way too much compared to their own internal world.

We cannot control our external environment and trying to all the time will only result in stress, frustration and an overall lack of inner self awareness.

People are influencing us all the time. They have made decisions for us and we have picked up certain habits from them during our lives that still affect us in many different ways.

External influences are constantly being accidentally let into our inner world without us even being aware of it. Starting from today, you must be the owner of your emotions and begin taking control of what outside influences mean to you.

Tom was a young man attending college. He fancied a girl in his business class. One day during lunch, he decided to pick up his courage to ask her out. As he walked across the lunch room he slowly approached her...

He failed to notice a lunch tray left on the floor in front of his feet - to which he slipped on his backside. Everybody in the cafeteria, including the girl he liked, pointed and laughed. Tom embarrassedly ran out of the cafeteria with baked beans down his ass. He has never felt comfortable and relaxed with women since.

This story illustrates that tom's external environment affected his self esteem in a major way.

If tom were more relaxed and realized that everyone was laughing with him; the experience would have been internalized in a beneficial way, since he would have found the situation amusing also, and maybe even as a means to become closer to the girl he liked.

Instead he was affected by the way how he internalized the entire situation. (Baked beans down his ass!)

External events influence us into feeling different emotions all throughout the day. We have arguments with people, something is spilled on the carpet and needs to be cleaned; maybe someone doesn't do what we ask of them or maybe someone says something to upset us.

Depending on how you personally internalize these different external experiences, will in turn affect your emotional state and future growth towards gaining higher self esteem.

Internal equals external

Earlier we discussed that Tom viewed his external world in a way that affected his higher self esteem.

The major reason why Tom's internal world was affected - was due to the way how he perceived his external environment in that particular moment. His internal thoughts and feelings that he created were not serving him in relation to what was happening within his surroundings.

When Tom fell over the lunch tray he didn't think to himself "Ha ha I fell over this is embarrassing ha ha" - in a way that made him feel good inside. Rather he thought to himself "Oh no I fell over in front of the girl I like and now she's laughing at me just like everybody else".

This direction in thinking affected his higher self esteem, due to his personal perception of what was happening within his environment at the time.

We usually react to our environment in a way that we are used to, and most of the time what we are used to, is not what we really want.

Are there any particular habitual reactions of thought, behaviours or feelings you may have towards your external environment that never seem to serve you?

Soon enough you will be learning how to get rid of them…

Internal world

Your internal world consists of your thoughts, opinions, beliefs, likes, dislikes, emotions etc - and how you feel about all these things overall.

Our self esteem **is** our internal reality.

During my low self esteem period I would sit in my room - In the dark, and continuously think about all the characteristics I hated about myself. I would regret the things I hadn't done; I would chastise myself continuously for how pathetic I was and also for how depressing my life was turning out. I created loops of negative attacking thoughts and feelings that would eventually lead to my doom in self esteem.

Your internal world is affected in a major way by what thought patterns you run on a daily basis.

What is so very useful about this is that we analyze ourselves, and then come up with overall opinions based on what we think about them. So if you begin to think in uplifting self empowering and positive directions you will experience the benefits of what this brings.

If you were to continuously think about all the beneficial qualities and possibilities that life has to offer. And begin to recognize that this allows you to feel good about yourself - you can notice your beginning to feel better already; only by the means of thinking about the thoughts that allow you to feel good in the first place.

You do possess the natural power to use this right now!

What most people do is sit around waiting for some external stimulus to kick them into action or to make them feel better. They forget we all have the natural ability to make ourselves feel motivated and uplifted anytime we want!

Trains of thought are easily created when you focus and then begin to get stuck into a new particular direction of thinking. Even if you don't believe what you are thinking about is necessarily true, you will still feel the emotions attached to these thoughts.

Imagine if all the feelings you have ever wanted suddenly became a part of your life right now; passion, excitement, love, happiness, motivation and inner strength. All due to you creating the thoughts that allow you to feel this way anyway.

All of these thoughts, feelings and self discoveries happen within your internal world and are yours to create and project towards your life. As you empower yourself and discover new directions of thinking that is always consciously targeted towards your personal growth, you can find your higher self esteem becoming more stronger from now on.

Be aware and notice

We must protect our internal world as to make sure we don't accept any outside influences that do not serve our higher self esteem.

During childhood when someone is bullied, they are not aware of the damaging effects that are caused within their internal world. They usually think in directions that pretty much accept all the negative influences that are presented. Then they go off rationalizing in ways that only makes them feel even worse!?

When people are not aware of what influences are being thrown their way, they can end up becoming victims of their own perceived environment, not to mention their own thoughts.

The thoughts we create are the feelings that come with it. The directions of thinking we actively use when a negative influence has been presented whether true or not will determine what the influence means to us.

If whenever you feel a down grading or hindering emotion you dislike. It is due to the trains of thought, reactions and reasons that you create that makes yourself feel bad. On some level you must begin to accept that you are the pilot who is meant to take control of the plane!

You must think in directions to discover the possibilities of redirection - enabling you to counteract the unbeneficial emotions and influences so they become untrue - or to find a beneficial alternative that serves you.

An example: "I am fat because I must learn how to become thin again" - Or from my own personal experience "No one likes me because I am unique in my own beneficial way that serves me" Or "I went through this awful experience to become stronger"

These reasons don't even need to be necessarily true just yet, as long as they contribute to your higher self esteem USE IT. You can make them as silly as you like and feel the pleasant experiences they bring.

Encourage yourself in absolutely any way you can think of to demonstrate to yourself that you are slowly becoming your own best friend.

Everything boils down to which trains of thought you are creating in reaction to external influences and what reasons you come up with in relation to them.

If you ever catch yourself attacking your self image, STOP! And begin to start creating new positive trains of thought that serve you. Your daily thoughts will always have some sort of an impact on your self worth, so use good empowering ones.

Begin to become aware of how you are thinking about yourself, your life and the people within it. And redirect these thoughts in a way that demonstrates you are supporting yourself - gradually becoming your own best friend!

In a nutshell

1. Your external environment consists of everything that is perceived to be outside of yourself

2. Your internal world consists of your thoughts and feelings within you (your self esteem)

3. Become aware of any negative thoughts or feelings that affect your self esteem; whether from external or internal and create positive thoughts and reasons that serve you within its place. No matter how silly they are purposely feel better in relation to them

4. React towards negative external influences with good intentions and empowering trains of thought that allow you to feel supported by your self image (If you do not feel like you are your own best friend when external negative influences come your way, you are using the wrong conclusions)

Understanding Self Esteem

Aggression

These days many of us experience forms of aggression on a daily basis. Sometimes this aggression can be so strong that we take it out on other people. This type of behaviour can affect everyone around you especially yourself since it hinders your own personal growth.

The particular people that possess aggressive qualities are trying to compensate for a lack of self esteem they do not have for themselves. They usually attempt to hold onto an aggressive stature to either protect their own self esteem despite others feelings or to gain a momentary compensation of pride because they cannot create good feelings within for themselves.

If positive feelings we experience are gained by means of attacking someone else we may not have the self esteem we truly need. You will eventually find yourself achieving higher self esteem when feelings are created by you within and have become a part of who you are.

Passiveness

Being passive can also cause us a lot of grief. Especially when we get upset over little subjects that when we really think about it, isn't really worth getting upset over.

Beating ourselves up over matters will in turn only cause self pity.

The most dangerous forms of passiveness that affect a persons self esteem are the thoughts, behaviours and feelings they use towards themselves. The only reason why people suffer from any form of low self esteem is because they beat themselves up about their insecurities in one area or another.

In any case, encouraging and supporting yourself to do better in those specific areas you need to, is the best way to go from now on.

Higher self esteem

People that 'naturally' have higher self esteem and confidence is usually fortunate enough to be brought up this way. But the downside to what these people have gained is if something very dramatic were to happen in their lives, it could cause them to lose their self esteem and confidence altogether; only due to the fact that they weren't aware of what or when it was happening in the first place.

Luckily for us we can begin learning the new techniques throughout this book that will enable us to become more aware of what is actually going on - and how to turn anything around for the positive.

You will not only gain supercharged self esteem but also learn how to keep it for the rest of your life.

Aggressive Taking advantage of others

Continuously betraying someone can result in that person eventually feeling they cannot trust you. Taking advantage of others also proves that you have low self esteem. Since you are using people to gain what you want out of life because you don't have the capability in creating it for yourself.

Passive Allowing people to take advantage of us

When you see a friend getting taken advantage of don't you feel like protecting them? You need to begin sticking up for yourself by holding onto positive feelings, and reject being affected by the negativity of others from this moment on. Start supporting and defending yourself as when you do this, you will find your self dignity returning to you.

Higher self esteem Standing up for your rights

We all have the right to stick up for ourselves and for what we believe in. Since we have these rights we must also respect the rights of other people likewise. We do not stick up for our rights in an aggressive or passive manner; rather we use a calm firm approach that is respectful when communicating our thoughts and opinions.

This will demonstrate to yourself and others that you possess a very calm and secure higher self esteem.

Aggressive Having no respect for others

Disrespecting people means we test their boundaries and do not respect their view of the world. Testing others boundaries is a purpose attempt to make people feel angry or upset, trying to blow things out of proportion when it comes to others hurts and frustrations. These are usually verbal attacks used to make people feel inferior.

People that attack others do this to gain a temporary sense of pride or phoney satisfaction, as they are searching for an external response to make themselves feel better. To put it simply, they can't make themselves feel good so they prey on others.

Having respect for yourself and others is one of the biggest representations of wisdom and maturity - and must not be taken lightly.

Passive Feelings of being socially inferior

If we practice unbeneficial patterns, we eventually get good at running them. This is what happens when we do not pay attention to ourselves and begin to recognize what's going on in our internal world.

When you begin to become aware of when inappropriate feelings pop, up you can discover the reasons behind what is fuelling them; you will then learn the positive aspects of the problem and how it has kept you safe to create new positive feelings that flow through you from now on.

Higher self esteem Respect yourself and other people.

Recognizing how you view yourself as a person and respecting yourself by acknowledging and constantly being aware of your self esteem. You are taking care and strengthening your internal world by setting out to make yourself feel good. When you are doing this you are becoming more of who you are and respecting the way how you feel, which represents you are sticking up for your emotions; in addition, this will also allow you to respect other people's emotions too.

You understand how to respect yourself and this helps you to understand how to respect others.

Aggressive wrap up

In essence no one is ultimately better than anybody else at all. We are all the same, with different life experiences, skills and feelings - unique in our own special way.

If you need to seek out the approval of others by boasting, bragging, being manipulative or proving to others for your **own** achievements - you do not possess the level of higher self esteem that you truly deserve. This is the lowest form of self appreciation for your achievements.

When you become truly confident within yourself there will be no need for you to show it to everybody. Confident people know they are confident; to them it's just naturally who they are as they live their daily lives. They don't need to 'fake it' they are naturally being confident and this confidence is expressed through who they are and what they achieve. Not by what they say and how they act.

If you have any aggressive qualities, consider this as an opportunity to become truly independent in your life, to learn and discover your natural inner sense of self wanting to be unleashed within you.

In a nutshell

1. Aggressive people pretend to have it all together by making others look inferior so they can look good

2. Aggressive people seek validation from others on one level or another, since they are incapable of truly validating themselves

3. Real self esteem and self assurance comes from within - and since it's already present, there is no need to prove it to others

Passive wrap up

The overall effect passive behaviour has on us is that we feel a low perception of ourselves for not thinking, behaving or feeling in the way we would like to. This makes us feel even worse because we know what problems we have; we want to fix them, but settle for less or feel too scared or hesitant to become more. This can lead to a cycle of disempowering thoughts, behaviours and feelings until we **STOP**! And begin moving in a positive direction that feels better.

Break out of negative loops and begin practicing to become the bearer of higher self esteem you rightfully deserve to be. Soon you will gradually find yourself beginning to unleash your true inner potential. You will begin to feel truly centred within yourself as you discover what else is possible in your life.

In a nutshell

1. Passive people tend to downgrade themselves or let others put them down

2. Break passive behaviour whenever you are aware of it to create new loops for ongoing higher self esteem

3. Begin to focus on what's empowering and uplifting; protect yourself from anything that stunts this wonderful growth of self assurance from now on!

Higher self esteem wrap up

People that possess higher self esteem feel self assured and confident in many areas of their lives and pursue to become more self assured in those specific areas which they at first find difficult. They go on an adventure - searching for challenging experiences that allow them to become more of who they are.

Higher self esteem allows you to feel a growing sense of self respect as you now focus on your beneficial qualities and experiences. As a result, you are respecting your feelings and this allows you to respect yourself. And you are respecting yourself by respecting your feelings.

So why not do this on a regular basis for yourself?

Now you know what you want, to become more of who you are in a growing and self fulfilling way.

In a nutshell

1. Higher self esteem allows you to have a mutual respect for yourself and others

2. Higher self esteem engages positive behaviours and forms of thinking that serve you

3. You will begin to feel more self assured and comfortable within yourself. Ready to take on those challenges that make you stronger as you continue growing in higher self esteem

Association and Dissociation

Not knowing the difference between association and dissociation is the main reason why most of us are not aware of our own thoughts, behaviours and feelings.

Most of us say things like "Other people are the only ones that can really see what I 'm doing on a daily basis, and that's why I lose track of my life!"

It maybe somewhat true that when you are engulfed in your feelings you may find it hard to view them objectively. Have you ever experienced a time when you did something without really considering your motives, and then lateron painfully regretted it?

Sometimes your emotions can take you away on what seems to be like a long rollercoaster ride. Then you eventually get off, finally being able to revaluate with "what on earth just happened here?"

It is very useful to understand the difference between association and dissociation, because it will enable you to distinguish the positive emotions you want to feel vs the negative emotions you don't wan to feel on a daily basis.

Now let's understand the difference:

Take a minute to imagine yourself riding in a rollercoaster. See yourself sitting in the front car, riding up and down

Now, make another picture of a roller coaster, but this time, do NOT see yourself in the picture. See it as if you were looking out of your own eyes, sitting in the roller car. Ride for a few moments.

Now, which one of those felt more real to you? The second one? When you're looking out through your own eyes you are associated with your feelings and the fullness of the experience.

Now take some time to step out of yourself again, and see yourself from an outside perspective going up and down. Notice yourself over there chewing away in enjoyment. In this case you have now dissociated and may notice the feelings aren't as strong as to when you were associated.

Dissociation

Dissociation is a great tool we can use to analyse our own aggressive and/or passive everyday behaviours, thoughts and feelings. And also enables us to deconstruct them, to find out the difference between what you want to keep and what mistakes you can learn from.

Taking a side step from the full experience is especially useful when you're feeling bad or having an argument.

Exercise

1. Remember a time when you acted or reacted in an aggressive or passive manner towards an outside influence and watch yourself going through this particular situation again

2. Now analyse from a perspective that allows you to come up with some ideas on what actions and meanings you could've used instead

You can use dissociation in many different perspectives that allows you to discover in many different ways. Just take some time to step out of yourself for a moment to view the negative situation objectively.

Association

Stepping into yourself allows you to fully gain comfort into your positive experiences. And as you feel them at a greater degree of intensity you become one with yourself and the feelings you are having.

This is a great tool we can use when we want to fully associate into the positive experiences we've had in the past or dreams, goals and impressions for the near future; you can also fully associate with the uplifting feelings you are experiencing right now to fully become one with this incredible moment!

Exercise

1. Imagine a time in the past were you felt really happy and fulfilled. What were you doing? What thoughts were you having? How were you moving your body? How were you feeling?

2. Take some time to really recognize how good it felt to feel 'oh so' good

3. Now fully associate into yourself and become one with this experience all over again; and notice how good you feel

Take time to flood yourself with positive scenarios and happy fulfilling moments.

Whenever you are feeling positive uplifting experiences, whether it being created or just generally felt within you, associate and own them as your own in a way that empowers you. And thank yourself for the fact that you can make yourself feel good.

Use dissociation anytime you are in a negative experience or have unwanted reactions to external influences. Just close your eyes for a second whenever you're having a bad experience and dissociate to analyse yourself in a way that serves you.

Practice these two to feel good about yourself - towards attaining higher self esteem and confidence.

In a nutshell

1. Dissociation is the act of viewing your situations objectively

2. Association is looking at the world through your own eyes; fully one with the experience

3. Step out of yourself to analyze the aggressive and/or passive behaviours, thoughts, feelings and reactions that don't serve you; and discover what new habits and daily patterns you can use to create a better future

4. Associate into your positive past, in the beneficial imagined future experiences you want to make part of your life. And associate into the empowering feelings you have in the present moment! Appreciate the fact that you can make yourself feel good by using your imagination

Uncovering your Inner Self

As humans we are generally taught to keep up with 'the trend' and respond to the environment like a herd of sheep or a bunch of mindless robots, rather than stopping for a moment to uncover what it is we deeply want to create in our lives.

Imagine if you lived your whole life up until now as a robot equipped with a learning chip, which enabled you to learn the negative thoughts, behaviours and emotional processes of general society. You did whatever you were told and learned habits according to your programmed acceptance.

Now consider the notion of you miraculously morphing from robot to human being, having the ability to realize you have ended up with numerous processes you do not want anymore. Would you keep them? How would you feel if you never had them in the first place?

When we are children we are spontaneous, full of life, freedom and joy. Everything is a big adventure full of possibility. At this stage we are new and free from societal limits. We are not concerned with being socially accepted and we tend to follow our own playful needs; until we are told to grow up and take on everyday societal problems such as; headaches, stress, tiredness and a overall lack of joy for living.

Living life with an opened sense of possibility and freedom is not a dream or something we can only experience as children. It is an overall attitude and an up to date way of perceiving life that you can connect with anew.

You are the owner of your life and the only one who can decide what is best for your growth; and its time to dig a little deeper - to uncover your individual inner sense of self. The self that is independent and free from disempowering limits and only going by what you personally believe is right for your life.

Spend a little time on each of the following questions and if you are having trouble answering them straight away; it means you are finally discovering what you truly want. So keep digging!

Am I thinking in a way that society has trained me to?

Am I behaving in a way that society has trained me to?

Am I feeling in a way that society has trained me to?

What would I need to posses or achieve in my physical environment to fill the emptiness within? How will this make me feel?

What would I need to encourage, motivate and praise myself about, on a daily basis to fill the emptiness within? How will this make me feel?

What disempowering thoughts do I have, that prevent me from filling the emptiness within? Why aren't they useful?

What kinds of thoughts will I be thinking if I already have filled the emptiness within? How does this make me feel?

What unbeneficial behaviours do I do, that prevent me from filling the emptiness within? Why aren't they useful?

What behaviours will I be doing if I already have filled the emptiness the within? How does this make me feel?

What useless feelings do I have, that prevent me from filling the emptiness within? Why aren't they useful?

What feelings will I be feeling if I already have filled the emptiness within? How does this make me feel?

Can I imagine what it will feel like, if my desired thoughts, behaviours and feelings were now already strengthened and acknowledged within me?

How do I think, behave and feel when I look back on this moment as having been the start of it?

Since I was once untamed by society's disempowering thoughts, behaviours and feelings shouldn't I have been like this anyway?

Is this inner realization my desired sense of self?

After you have pealed away and uncovered the outer layers of the orange_ you will eventually find the juice and the source of what feels good deep inside.

Your inner self is unique and you generally have five important human needs to fulfil this untapped place within you.

<u>Peace - Love - Happiness - Power - Success</u>

Strengthening your five human needs - will enable you to become centred with what it is you really deserve.

Peace

You want to feel comfortable, secure, relaxed, and possess a life that is stress free and this is a human need; to be at peace as you experience a sense of freedom from all worries.

Love

Love is a human need and you can build on self love allowing you to spread love and connection with yourself, friends, family and your ideal lover. Humans naturally feel and need love, connection and passion, and this is what makes your life extra special.

Power

We all want to feel strong inside, motivated, sexy and confident and this is a human need; to grow in a powerful way that truly benefits your life and becoming secure and centred within.

Happiness

Laughter, joy, excitement and happiness; if we didn't have these uplifting emotions, life wouldn't feel like life. These emotions keep us vitalized and happiness makes life fun and fulfilling.

Success

Success in every area of your life is what you're here for; whether it's in family life, friends, your career, marriage and most of all - the feelings of success you feel for yourself.

Imagine what it will feel like if your five needs were strengthened inside of you right now. You will have everything you need to be in touch with yourself to be abundant in life.

You will discover the undeniable power of your natural growing higher self esteem, unleashing the unshakable need to grow and become more of who you are - making your five human needs a natural part of your everyday being.

Exercise

Do this exercise!

1. Take some time to form a ball in your hands with some values of peace, love, happiness, power and success. (You should now have a ball in your hands with all these emotional needs you desire to feel for yourself)

2. As you hold it in your hands - notice what colour it is glowing

3. Throw the ball in the air and catch it a couple of times to gain a sense of its emotional value

4. Go to that place within you that is hurting inside or needs more out of life. Place your ball inside of this area as you take in a deep breath

5. Now ask this new feeling inside "Can you share your wonderful feelings with me?" And feel, listen and gain a sense of a voice coming from this place saying "yes, I will always be there for you"

As you practice and spend some time to become re-acquainted in this mutual respect of needing your renewed inner self, you will gain a sense of harmony spilling out into every area of your life.

YOUR INNER SELF **IS** YOUR FIVE HUMAN NEEDS. AND THEY ARE NOW PLEADING WITH YOU TO CONNECT WITH THEM!

Say this to yourself: "They are now pleading me to connect with them"

Answer to your inner self's love, peace, happiness and power from within, as you grow in the life success that you deserve to feel inside.

Your inner self is always within you waiting to offer an experience of inner comfort, centeredness and peace.

In a nutshell

1. Notice your inner self is a place where your love, peace, happiness power and success is always available for you to experience within

2. We all have this place within, and will be unlocked when you uncover your true inner desires of wanting to become more

3. Create a mutual - strong agreement and bond with this empowering place within until it feels natural for you to feel good about yourself (You will know when this has happened)

Tips: If you like, you could talk and listen to the pleasant voice that comes from this place, as this place is always encouraging and reminding you that you already have everything you need inside. Communicate and grow in your bond, and be thankful that the inner you always responds to you in an uplifting way

Take your attention off this place for a second and then acknowledge this place again as if you are missed by your inner self

Experiment in any way that allows you to gain rapport with your inner self.

To become completely empowered you must "become one" with your inner self. To do this you must "need to". The more you need this feeling the more you will draw closer to it and the more it will draw closer to you; eventually becoming a natural part of your everyday life.

PART TWO

TAKING CONTROL

The Mind

Many people are led to believe we only have one mind; the mind is actually made up of two parts, the conscious mind and the unconscious mind. These two parts of the mind make up our one mind.

The conscious mind - is literally **you** in this moment. Whatever, thoughts, and actions you actively use right now is based upon your awareness and decision to do so. If you didn't have your conscious mind you wouldn't be able to communicate or even move your body.

The unconscious mind learns and remembers your conscious experiences. It possesses billions of interconnecting neuro pathways which make up the map for your general life's understanding. It is constantly responding with multiple ideas, thoughts and feelings simultaneously and is aware of what you do in the present moment.

The purpose of the conscious mind then - is to give direction to the unconscious and to condition, programme or teach in what you want it to learn, in terms of the thoughts and behavioural patterns you desire. So it can respond positively with your active experience.

When learning to drive a car for the first time it can be difficult to push the pedal, turn the wheel, look where you're going, indicate...etc, all at the same time, since you are only able to consciously focus on one to two subjects at a time.

With practice though, the unconscious frees up your active mind by learning the thoughts and behaviours needed for the once daunting task and then processes them automatically for you.

This enables you to listen to music and admire the scenery without having to put your full attention on everything else.

The behaviours and thoughts that you have learned up until now that you don't want - are only habitual by means of your accidental past learning's being processed by your unconscious.

Don't you think its time to improve and unlearn those useless habits you don't want?

The conscious mind

The conscious mind is the totality of this moment that you are in right now.

You may round this up based upon the constant internal voice you may refer to as "me".

You can be aware and attentive of your environment, your thoughts, behaviours and feelings. You experience complete freedom of choice in this moment to focus, move and take action upon whatever you decide to.

You can do just about anything you choose right now. From running around the streets naked, to diving through a bullet proof window, TO MAKING THE DECISION THAT YOU ARE NOT WILLING TO SETTLE FOR ANYTHING LESS THAN YOU CAN BE!

You have the freedom of choice!

Reaching out to point at something or to tell the time, is a decision made that requires your conscious attention. Recalling a past memory also **first** requires your conscious attention, to <u>choose</u> what you would like to remember.

Your conscious mind is in action when you decide, move, make choices, have desires and communicate with people.

The unconscious mind

The unconscious (the larger part of the mind) stores your entire past within its memory database. Its main function **is** memory, storing up all the information that makes you up today as a person, and this enables you to remember your entire life experience.

It reasons like a computer drawing conclusions from your conscious experiences, remembering them, and then bringing them back up to your awareness whenever you need to remember a specific thought or memory.

To remember anything you must first access your memory (your unconscious mind)

Take some time to answer these questions to gain a better understanding. What colour is your door? Do you like fish? What type of music do you like? What does it sound like?

To answer these questions you must remember them.

Your unconscious is built upon your memories.

Whatever has been previously learnt during your past; hindering thoughts, behavioural patterns and feelings will continue to run automatically until you renew your intend towards consciously creating something new.

A person that has a major fear of flying has come up with reasons and meanings for why flying is a fearful experience. These feelings, thoughts and behaviours automatically show up whenever the subject of flying comes up again, so they usually go back into their fearful state.

People in general tend to not be aware of their own thoughts, behaviours and feelings and worse, ignore them completely and irresponsibly let them spiral out of control; they think they cannot change or learn better alternatives. But we can, just as we are now learning new things all the time. And when you begin to realize that all of those disempowering habits were just accidentally learned by the unconscious anyway, you can find yourself feeling a growing sense of self assurance; you can begin to practice and learn the new positive thoughts and behaviours you want to.

The Mind

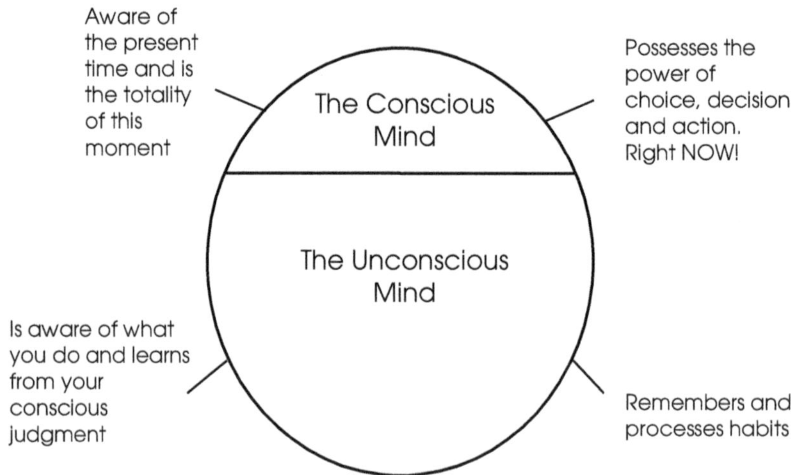

In a nutshell

1. The unconscious picks up on your conscious reasoning

2. Your unconscious learns, and then reacts in response to what you are consciously attentive of in the moment

3. Your conscious mind is the decider and teacher (You)

4. You have the ability to decide, behave and reason in directions that now serve you

Accepting Where You Are Now

The reason why most people have lost their self esteem, confidence, happiness, self worth...etc, is because they are not consciously aware of the effects as to what is really going on in their lives.

We tend to be so wrapped up in our daily lives that we ignore our emotions, thoughts and behaviours until later we come realize that we have a bag of habits and patterns that we do not want. And worse than that, didn't even know how they got there in the first place!

We must begin to respect ourselves by monitoring our emotions, thoughts and behaviours regularly so we can keep track and discover what is missing within our lives.

It's not your fault that you were not aware of the unlimited resources you truly possess. When growing up we are not usually taught how to gain emotional self control, but as you are learning this, you can decide to take control or your life RIGHT NOW.

A big step in beginning to get rid of useless emotions and strengthening positive emotions is by first accepting them both as your own.

This will enable you to discover where you are in your life right now as opposed to where you desire to be.

Take a minute to answer each following question and be honest with yourself:

1. How do you feel on a daily basis?

2. How did you feel yesterday?

3. If you continue to do what you're doing now, where will you be 5 years from now?

4. Which types of negative emotions will you like to change?

5. What's stopping you from getting what you desire?

6. What do you want to be successful at in your life?

7. What will drive you to succeed when going after what you desire?

Exercise

1. Close your eyes

2. Dissociate from yourself for a moment and analyse who you are and what you do on a daily basis

3. What doesn't serve me? What am I really like? What energies do I project to others in my life? What will this result in if I continue? If I continue behaving in this way, where will I be 5 years from now? Do I really want this?

Figure out what kinds of habits you want to gain, and the habits you want to get rid of. These habits whether empowering or disempowering are a part of you, and they won't change until you now accept them and decide **you** deserve so more for yourself.

I don't know where you are in your life right now. You could be feeling somewhat low, relatively fine or even at the top of your game; but wherever you are its time to push yourself to a new higher level of growth.

Remember; you are in control of the plane and must accept your life for the way it currently is, so you can now make better choices and find yourself growing stronger in higher self esteem.

If by strange circumstances you had to fly a plane because the pilot jumped out and left you on your own, would you gawp at the controls or take control to save yourself from crashing?

Take note of where you are in your life on a daily basis, so you can find new ways on how to feel better from today ongoing.

Take some time to discover what kind of person you are, who you really want to become and what kind of life you choose to lead.

After all, this is your life! What in this world is more important than your life? If you didn't have it, you wouldn't have anything!

Buy a journal, record yourself and spend some quiet time with yourself daily. It doesn't matter what keeping track means to you. Just do it!

Your days are built and created by your daily decisions and actions. Keep track of your progress as you are growing in higher self esteem, and find yourself strengthening desires and/or replacing the flaws you didn't want.

In a nutshell

1. Regain control by accepting where you are currently and never lose track of any ongoing process until it is achieved

3. Set out to discover yourself inwards, to spark up positive states and new ideas to unleash your inner sense of self.

Habitual thoughts, behaviours and emotions

Positive and negative habits alike are both learned by you. Your unconscious never argues with what you continue to persist in practicing. It learns what you learn and what you generally accept as being true.

There are many positive habitual thoughts and behaviours in which we can choose to learn and practice within our daily lives. After all, the useless daily patterns you were running before were also previously practiced and learnt.

Knowing those old patterns do not serve you, it is time to make some new discoveries and new decisions that create a brighter future.

Imagine what it would feel like if you automatically possessed the positive thoughts, behaviours and feelings within you, every minute of the day that consistently jump from one uplifting experience to the next.

There are trillions of new possibilities that lay within your unconscious, and you can discover in many new directions according to what you desire, as you gradually open yourself up to the new experiences.

Many other people have learned to do so; it's your time now.

In a nutshell

1. Your unconscious learns, and then processes any, if not every habit or pattern that you discover and practice in

2. The possibilities for creating the life you deserve is infinite and this power lies right between your ears, entirely yours to use at will

The conscious teaches

Someone that is very successful in a particular area of life is usually a result of them consistently focusing on the benefits of their actions in the short and long term. As a result, they continuously renew their decisions to use their daily focus and actions, to improve in that specific area of life until they reach their given result.

This is a great benefit to us; the ability to teach the unconscious what we desire just by doing so.

The longer you focus; constantly renew your decisions and continue to affirm something, the more important your unconscious will regard it to be.

Setting small victories maybe what is required <u>at first</u> to take the initial steps forward that are suitable for you, as long as you continue taking these conscious steps forward you will always grow to feel good.

Focus on empowering thoughts and behaviours to feel little special moments of achievement. And you will eventually reach a point where you can't help yourself wanting to experience them again and again.

It's time to BECOME ONE with what you truly desire.

<u>In a nutshell</u>

1. The unconscious learns and you have the ability to teach it

2. Continue to affirm and renew your beneficial decisions to change your life for the better in numerous times of the day

3. You have the wonderful and amazing gift of consciousness to heighten your self esteem and confidence ongoing, so USE IT!

Take Control of Aggression

Are you angry at yourself or at others for the way things are?

Many people seem to think that anger is a sign of strength or power, but this is simply not true.

What anger really represents is a lacking of emotional control

A couple that were living together absolutely hated their jobs. They both became very stressed in their working environments and used to look forward to coming home to each other, but now all they seem to do is argue.

At work, they find their environments stressful to cope with as they can never get their own way, and so "getting their own way" becomes something to seek out else where, whether if it's having control of the TV remote, or manipulating or violating each others feelings.

They are the ones that can't **handle** the pressure, and this makes them angry.

This is a form of self deprivation, since they are ignoring their own problems by accepting their own flaws and weaknesses and being too ignorant to acknowledge and strengthen them within.

Having no inner control is something that is despised by every one of us.

We cannot be flawless in everything we do, and when we get upset or angry about things we have already lost control, because we have allowed an external influence to effect and bombard our brains; rather than controlling ourselves and staying focused and clear headed.

Aggression and passiveness are opposites but are the same, as they are both triggered in the exact same way. They **only** have different outcomes and effects.

Imagine a passive and aggressive person were put in a room together, with somebody else screaming offensive comments at them for 5 days. You will find that the aggressive and passive person both lose control in one way or another by either being offended or outraged.

When we are hurt we respond passively or aggressively. **When we are not hurt, we are calm.**

The key here, is to find that middle ground

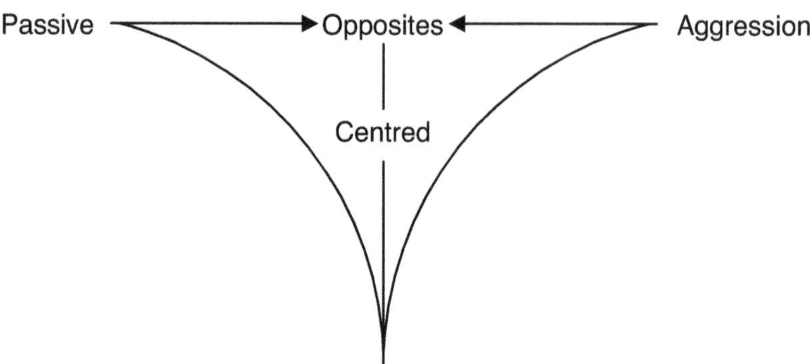

Find the inner control and balance within; To become emotionally abundant, self assured, and confidently centred within your ability to succeed and grow in higher self esteem.

Take some time to answer these questions:

What situations do you have trouble putting up with?
What are the weaknesses you have for why you can't deal with them within yourself?
What is missing inside for you to gain calm inner control?
What will it feel like if you already had calm inner control?

A good way to release the anger that you may have is to admit your own flaws. And view it as a piece of emotion that doesn't work by being determined to change it now.

This way you release the anger, while fixing the problem

This is only directed at reforming your weaknesses and not at yourself in any way that makes you feel inferior, or an attempt to put yourself down.

We are actually never perfect in life anyway and never will be - since as humans we are continuing to raise our standards to grow and become more. After all, if you were to obtain perfection wouldn't you still want more? In the end, driving yourself towards wanting **more** will only make you grow stronger - even if perfection cannot "really" be achieved.

Be determined to fix your own weaknesses by releasing the anger as useless wasted energy to gain a sense of inner control and vitality.

You will be able to stay calm in times of being manipulated or attacked and also become centred within your capability to manage your emotions.

Exercise

(Take some time on each section)

1. List and recognize all the weaknesses that make you feel incapable of staying calm. Admit and accept that you own them and don't want them any longer

2. Release your anger by screaming, shouting, throwing tantrums and do whatever you do to be angry at the fact that, you have flaws that your hinder success

3. Finally turn your flaws into determination to resolve the pursuit of achieving your beneficial goals

Be angry at the fact you DON'T have emotional abundance. After all, this is the real thing we should all be angry about; NOT HAVING EMOTIONAL CENTRED EMPOWERMENT.

Are you going to put up with being flawed and having a weak sense of inner control or balance?

Release your anger out for the fact that people **can** manipulate your inner sense of control, and be determined to **correct** your own flaws by becoming stronger within, and non-effected by external influences in a way that radiates like never before.

STOP REACTING TO EXTERNAL RESPONSE AND GAIN THE INNER CALM SELFASSURANCE AND FULLFILMENT THAT YOU CRAVE IN LIFE.

TRUE power comes from within to experience a **calm** inner balance! Use your lack of control to remind you of the control you don't have and be determined to correct it.

In a nutshell

1. Aggressive and passiveness are opposites but are on the same spectrum, as they are both triggered by the same influences. True power is keeping calm, in-control of your emotions and keeping a clear head

3. The anger you have about things is rooted deep in relation to what you are missing within

4. Release your anger and strengthen those weaknesses by directing your determination towards gaining inner management over your emotions

Forgive Yourself

The feelings that we do not want are past learning's - to which they **are** in the **past**. We cannot change the past and hanging onto disempowering experiences does not serve our higher self esteemed future.

Some people blame themselves for past mistakes and accidentally strengthen feelings of guilt, blame or incapability. They in a sense charge and fuel negative reasoning and this doesn't help in anything.

If you want to become stronger for the future is blaming your past going to help?

All you are really blaming is recalled experiences from the inside of your own head.

If we do this we accidentally practice incorrect habits of recalling these feelings and then blaming them for our incapability to change; Even though the past represents what we **have** done - and isn't as important as what we are doing **now** and **will** be doing to succeed in the future.

People like this tend to think "Why did I have to go through this?" "I hate this person for making me feel this way" "Why am I so pathetic?" Making false accusations towards ourselves will only make us feel even more incapable and depressed. You are in a sense attacking your self, what kind of a person are you anyway?

You want the best for you - but when you blame and accuse yourself, you will feel blamed and accused. This will only make you feel **confused**.

You want to **strengthen** the connection that you have with your unconscious, NOT diminish it.

Forgiving yourself for those past mistakes is a great first step into cutting away from them. When you are forgiven by someone you become free of guilt and burden - as you can now move on with your life freely into the near future.

Can you recall a time when you made someone feel bad while not meaning to? You then asked for their forgiveness, and once they forgave you - you were free to move on from the situation peacefully.

Exercise

Here is an exercise that you can do to experience freedom from past guilt

1. Remember a time when you did or felt something that made you feel guilty or stuck

2. Close your eyes and imagine yourself dissociated from the situation and gain a sense of how the past you felt at the time

3. Notice your past self in this situation forgiving you for what happened

4. Now step into yourself and feel comfortable with these feelings of forgiveness for yourself

When you release the guilt from the past you, you both become relaxed for the future. You know you have forgiven the old you and this means you are now forgiven also. As the past you have already forgiven you, you are also up until now forgiven too. And that feels better doesn't it?

Get used to the feelings of forgiveness from your past as this allows you to experience a release of freedom and energy for your upcoming future.

Forgiving breathing exercise

1. Take in a deep breath

2. Breathe out and feel a feeling of forgiveness flowing through you

3. Release yourself from past mistakes

Repeat this up to 4-8 times.

Feel free from what was once holding you back.

In a nutshell

1. The negative past represents what you HAVE been through and is not a part of the beneficial choices you are making right now

2. You want the best for you, so forgive yourself for those past mistakes, learn from them and release yourself freely into the future you are creating

It becomes attached

People become attached to the way how they do things since they become used to doing what they are used to doing.

Have you ever had an experience where you were so used to doing something so often, that when someone came along and told you to do it in a new way, you found it somewhat difficult to change?

This is because we become comfortable with running our 'run in the mill' habits; so much so that when we want to go about things in a new way, we become challenged as we already possess reasons as to why we do what we do currently.

It's a shame negative feelings that hold us back don't just go away with a snap of a finger. The unconscious can be pretty much bashful in the same way as a computer can only carry out the processes it has been programmed.

It's not until you continue to affirm what you want that you begin to gradually grow and become what you want.

We all have particular emotions and blocks in life that we do not want from this moment on. But since the unconscious has become attached to your normal everyday patterns, you must now consciously become attached to discovering new patterns that personally serve you. You will gain a positive fulfilling connection with your desires as you grow together with this new feeling throughout your life instead.

The limits that hold us back, held by the unconscious is like a wild bird trapped in a cage. When you keep presenting and focusing on the new positive feelings that you desire in life, you begin to grow attached to what you truly desire. The cage will open and the bird will grow calmer and eventually fly out into freedom.

In a nutshell

1. Stop trying to hang onto self damaging thoughts, behaviours and feelings you don't want.

2. The unconscious becomes attached to what you are aiming to achieve. Set yourself free to wonder towards the future you deserve

Focus and concentration

A major talent that you possess is that of having the ability to concentrate. And this allows you to <u>focus</u> with **precision**.

When we become aware of our surroundings our awareness is somewhat like being in a dark room with a torch that enables us to gain a sense of our environment.

Concentration however, is an act of using <u>directed focus</u>. Almost like a laser beam directed at a specific desired target or outcome.

When we concentrate we use the <u>totality</u> of our consciousness. This allows us to figuratively step into what our attention is directed upon.

When you use your focused laser beam and aim it in the benefiting directions of achieving your goals, empowering feelings arise in relation to conscious attention. You virtually feel good right now just by focusing on it.

You can also concentrate and practice in things that do not even exist yet. For example: practice in feeling like a success in a way that allows you to feel you are **already** a success. With this talent you can create literally anything you desire to put your mind to. The unconscious responds to **you**, not the other way round.

Some people make the big mistake in acting according to what old patterns the unconscious has been running for years. Others assume that when a negative feeling arises they should act according to it and this is a HUGE misunderstanding in general society.

<u>You were meant to be the master as you possess the power of choice, decision, desire, focus and action.</u>

When you focus on what it feels like to <u>already</u> have obtained the empowering daily patterns you desire, doesn't it seem you were <u>already</u> practicing them all along?

Choose to focus and make the conscious decisions to practice in growing <u>used to</u> achieving your goals.

In a nutshell

1. Focus and concentration allows you to step into your desired experiences

2. Your unconscious mind is subject to you; so be a leader of what you consider to be beneficial in your life

3. Set out to become one with what you deserve, in a way that allows you to feel like it has **already** happened

Taking Responsibility

Taking responsibility for our thoughts and behaviours is the one key rule we need to use and learn to gain more control of our lives.

If we don't then who will?

You must use your natural abilities of awareness, focus, choice and action in the creation of your aspiring future.

We all run patterns that we do not want. But the main question we miss asking ourselves is: How do we stay in control and get rid of them?

If you had been aware of your emotions from the day you were able to walk and chose to discard the emotions you didn't want, and strengthened and created the emotions you now **do** want. How different do you think you would be feeling right now?

Now that you know this, what are you going to do from now on? **Maybe** the whole world should start teaching their children this; to take responsibility for our daily thoughts and emotions.

What is taking responsibility?

According to the Collins Dictionary and Thesaurus *Express 2005*

Taking is to: Conduct, escort, lead, acquire, bring about and guide.

Responsibility is: Having control and authority, you are answerable and accountable

Our senses and natural abilities of choice and action are wonderful gifts of self control and power that we as humans already possess.

Believe it or not, you once possessed full control over your life you just didn't know how to use it.

I can personally recall a time when I was 6 years old. My mum would tell me "You can achieve anything you put your mind to!" But yet a simple phrase would pass me as I continued to live naive and oblivious as to what was **really** going on. I had all the resources, excitement, joy and freedom we all alike had at that age but just didn't know how to **use it**.

It's time to start bringing about the control in your life you once had!

Blaming somebody else

Blaming somebody else for what we may **think** we have lost or can't obtain is a common mistake among people. Depending on how long we choose to blame others, will determine how long we have **mistakenly** offered somebody else our potential power.

Getting to that point of blaming somebody else can happen in a numerous of ways and your responsibility can sometimes wonder off into different places.

About two years ago I was in a relationship with a girl I really liked. I eventually began to like her so much that I continuously accepted verbal abuse from her. At first I didn't care and found a reason to ignore it. As I continued to focus on this, it only made me like her even more despite all the bitchiness I was taking!

Anyway, sooner rather than later she dumped me! She even went back out with me and then dumped me again!

I eventually stamped the label on my head reading "certified loser" and found it hard to develop new relationships after that and blamed my ex for the mistrustful feelings I experienced towards commitment.

However, soon after I began to realize that THE ONLY PERSON I HAD TO BLAME WAS MYSELF. I should have taken responsibility and should've been aware of when that devil woman was hijacking my emotions.

Silly me, I wasn't aware and allowed her to do extreme damage to me; even though she probably wasn't aware of the effects it was having on me herself. (Silly girl)

REALIZE that the past is out of your life right now, and you're not going to let ANYTHING ruin your future. What would be the point in blaming the way how you used to feel? When you are truly <u>responsible</u> and have the <u>choice</u> in being able to <u>decide</u> what NOT to settle for in your life RIGHT NOW, from **this moment on**.

If you blame someone else for a self deprecating feeling that **you** are <u>choosing</u> to hold onto, then that would mean you expect **them** (other people) to do something about it.

IT'S NOT THEIR FEELINGS THOUGH; IT'S YOURS!

They are not responsible for YOUR OWN FEELINGS. They **'could'** help; but what are <u>**you**</u> going to do about your future?

Knowing that you now know this, who should **take control**?

You have the responsibility to take control of your emotions. You can find yourself growing in creating the stronger feelings inside of you.

By blaming somebody else we automatically hand our self respect on a platter. The person who we are blaming, depending on what they do now, will determine how they make us feel in the near future. This gives them full control over our emotions and signifies we are respecting somebody else's opinions more than our own. OPEN YOUR EYES!

Don't be a real IDIOT like I was. Don't blame somebody else or come up with stupid reasons for why you think it's their fault. If you do this then you are purposely choosing to sabotage your own future. You are literally choosing to blame others so you can have an excuse to not take responsibility.

Become aware of your new found responsibility that benefits your emotional future; you have now opened another door for you to continue growing in higher self esteem - stronger than ever before as you regain your personal self control.

By using your responsibility in conjunction with your thoughts and actions, you are cutting off from negative chains that **were** once holding you back. This sets you free in discovering how to grow towards a stronger inner sense of self confidence.

Blaming your past

The biggest and most ultimate mistake we make that holds us back from gaining what we want is that we blame our **past** experiences and memories.

Now sometimes a person can be living a relatively happy life. Everything is going well and then all of a sudden a big tragedy happens that rocks their world. After this occurs the person may find it difficult to move on because they cannot stop thinking about it....

After an entire seven years later this person is still hanging onto it!?

It's a shame this person cannot move on by consciously focusing and practicing on the wonders of their potential future.

Sometimes it can be hard to let go, but you must realize that if you don't, your past will haunt you forever.

MOVING ON REPRESENTS WHAT YOUR LIFE IS GOING TO **BECOME**, NOT WHAT YOUR LIFE **ONCE** WAS

When it comes to blaming our pasts, we are only blaming memories by recalling them, analyzing them and coming up with overall opinions based on what they mean to us.

The meanings you have for these are to be reformed into empowering meanings that allow you to move on. Consider the fact that you once had a **new** experience and can now be the first to discover new empowering leaning's; growing to become a self made master of handling situations better if they were to ever happen again.

Think of some reasons for why negative experiences HAVE benefited you... Everything you have been through in your life up until now is the source towards gaining your unique personal wisdom.

Disempowering negative feelings have benefited me in miraculous ways; otherwise you wouldn't be reading this book!

Unbeneficial experiences that were new at the time were only accidentally handled in a way that wasn't serving you in that **past** particular moment.

You weren't aware of what was going on **then**, but you can be aware of what is going on **right now**.

CUT OFF FROM YOUR UNDESIRABLE PAST! The past consists of only memories, and **does not** equal the future.

Imagine the negative past being like a giant slug on your back, leaving a trail of slime that you continue to go back and suck on. Are you sick enough to continue looking back, sucking down on negative sludge? You know it's disgusting, so don't do it!

Hanging onto the negative past **is like** sucking on the slime the negative snail leaves behind you. Cut off from this slime ONCE AND FOR ALL! (I'm serious about this). Your negative sludge past **is** behind you forever! And your new empowering fruitful future is constantly being created as you read this.

Create and practice being in control of your destiny towards attaining higher self esteem.

A word about miracles

Luck is described as something fortunate that happens in our lives.

I'm sure you have heard of the woman that is in a popular and busy location minding her own business - then a photographer all of a sudden notices her. She then becomes a star in as little as a month. She makes loads of money all due to that one day she was out on the town shopping for a new skirt!?

How often does this happen? Not often enough it seems like for most of us.

Luck doesn't happen often enough and is a pointless waste of time to hope something wonderful will appear out of thin air.

SITTING AROUND HOPING FOR WHAT YOU DESIRE - WILL **NOT** GET YOU WHAT YOU WANT.

If hoping is all it took, we would all be successful by now!

Miracles are described as miraculous magical events that happen and just feel so wonderful - that you are forced to say the words "It's a miracle!"

The story of Jake

Jake was very depressed and didn't think much of himself or his life. He was often times very sad and felt sorry for himself on a daily basis.

One day he began to wonder how his life ever became so glum. He began to get fed up with the way his life was and decided to make a shift. He took responsibility that day by making the decision, to not settle for anything less than he could be and to demand more from himself.

Jake desperately wanted his desired reality to become real - real enough for him to see it, touch it and feel it surging through him.

He forced himself to take action everyday to change his life for the better, or die trying in the process. He started going out and meeting new people, forcing himself to feel happy even though he originally felt down. He drives himself beyond the limits he **once** thought were impossible, and he gradually begins to grow stronger. Eventually something clicks inside of him to which he realized that he has been reborn. "This is a miracle!" he thought to himself. As he reflects back he knows he has gained all of these new positive emotions due to one decision that he made, **to take responsibility and control of his own life.**

This is the way how **you** can make miracles happen **in your own life.**

The fact that the miracle will be all due to your own efforts makes you feel even better. Not to mention, the uplifting growing process you will be experiencing, as you are working your way towards your dreams becoming your desired reality.

The harder you go after what you desire in life, the faster it will become part of your daily existence. This will truly be a miracle, which you can appreciate within due to your very own efforts.

Now focus, behave and feel in terms of the miraculous future you are creating; as you do this you will feel more motivated to chase after it, excessively filling yourself up with a passion of living.

Miracles WILL happen!

After you have made the decision in using your responsibility in co-ordination with your actions - your self miracle will draw closer to you. You will soon enough achieve what you have been yearning for. You can then look back on this moment and giggle with the satisfaction that represents you are the creator of your new reality. All due to the fact **you have taken** your glorious uplifting future into your own hands.

Become a role model for yourself in your life and direct in the ways that are appealing to you.

In a nutshell

1. Blaming somebody else or blaming your past, gives away your responsibility and power of being in control of your life

2. Do not rely on others; rather be a leader and example of what success really represents to you for your future

3. Owning your responsibility signifies you are the creator of the self miracles you create in your life. Miracles will happen as you are the observer of them

It's not out to get you

Your unconscious is always trying to help and protect you. It keeps you safe by keeping you away from those assumed painful experiences, and tries to keep you away from what you view to be 'uncomfortable' until taught otherwise.

Your unconscious is like a servant helping you in a hidden way. If you desire to take action but feel uncomfortable, it's just a self defence mechanism.

Are you doing your job properly to condition your unconscious otherwise to obtain the emotional abundance you truly want?

Your unconscious is waiting to gain rapport with you so it can begin to learn the beneficial habits according to what **you** desire. It really does want to experience a sense of being at peace with you, and you do to.

When you begin to ponder in this, you are already becoming closer to the happiness you want to experience within. Give your mind something empowering to remember that allows you to feel at peace with yourself. And **realize** there is an inner comfort you are gradually growing in harmony within.

In a nutshell

1. Your unconscious is not against you; it only keeps you safe and learns what you teach it

2. Your mind's learning's and processes are infinite and is seeking to be in harmony with you, so set out to manifest this inner peace of mind

Choice

Can you remember when you were a child gazing upon thousands of sweets sparkling before your eyes? You were filled with excitement and amazement of the large amount of choice you had to indulge in.

This freedom of choice is available in every area of life RIGHT NOW!

There are **NO** restrictions in any way to choose, grow and accomplish in anything you want.

Right now you have the choice to become a famous celebrity. You have the choice to become more confident than George Bush. You have the choice to build a house from scratch. And you have the choice to manifest into the person you dream to be. You are human just like everyone else. The only difference is that some of us use and make better choices than others.

Some choose to steal, some choose to take positive action and some choose to do nothing about their lives at all. What choices are staring you in the face right now that you want to manifest in?

Realize that if you don't use choices to benefit your life, you have already made a choice to settle for less. Choice is available to you everywhere you go so use it actively to your advantage.

When you think about the choice you have between experiencing positive emotions next to negative emotions, which one do you like to choose every time? POSTITIVE EMOTIONS DON'T YOU!?

Base your life's choice on this understanding to choose whatever allows you to feel good!

Choose to open up to choice. Choose to take those actions that allow you to grow stronger. Choose to attain higher self esteem and choose to change your life right now!

Use unlimited choice and possibility as being a natural part of your daily awareness and you will manifest in what has naturally been available to you all along.

In a nutshell

1. Imagine the choices you have in life as if you were a kid in a candy store all over again

2. You have the choice to manifest in absolutely anything you want!

3. Adopt the freedom of choice into your life to release yourself into the land of unlimited possibility

Do This for You

When we don't change for ourselves, problems may arise that can prevent us from changing for the better; or even result in us growing and then going back to how we used to feel.

Changing for somebody else

Reforming for somebody else means that people are changing to meet somebody else's needs rather than their own. This means they give others full credibility for their hard work and accomplishments.

Changing completely for somebody else's beliefs and wants is not a very good reason for us to change. Because we could make the mistake of putting in big effort for somebody else to be proud of us; and this may result in us missing out on feelings of being proud of ourselves.

According to the Collins dictionary and thesaurus *express 2005*

Changing means to: Restyle, innovate, reform, a difference and revolution.

When you grow FOR YOURSELF, this self appreciation allows you to realize that when you take actions in co-ordination with your own desires, it will make YOU feel a rise in value, FOR YOU!

You can then take full credibility for your raise in security without having to think things like, "without this person I wouldn't be able to do this".

Instead you will be saying to yourself, "Thank you Nick (or whatever your name is) you've done well for yourself". This contributes to **your** own growing self esteem, NOT for the sake of somebody else's.

This does not mean we can't learn from people. It means we must be careful of succumbing to a persons will; because if that person were to betray or fall out with us for whatever reason, it could lead us into going back to our old negative thinking and behavioural patterns. After all, your positive associations for what you have gained may go, if that person takes their love and connections away from you as well.

Instead of restyling for someone else, ask for their support in you making the changes for yourself. This way you hold onto your own self appreciation to learn from them, **for you!**

You will have the support of close friends and family to cheer you on and motivate you to **do this for you.**

Certain people may not want you to change

Now, there are some people out there that may not want you to change or even during your positive growing process people may say "I don't like who you are becoming". These people are usually afraid of losing the person they are used to experiencing a certain connection with.

When you are growing in higher self esteem, you will begin to notice you are expressing your personality easily - feeling motivated each day and growing to become more self assured and happy.

Friends that are so used to you being a certain way, maybe slightly 'iffy' with your restyling and may feel like they are losing their <u>once</u> low self esteemed buddy.

This is a good thing; it proves that you are feeling so good about yourself that people are beginning to notice as it shines on the outside. Ironically other people may notice the positive changes before you do.

You are doing this for **you**, and as long as you are beginning to feel better within yourself, your friends will understand and may want to join in your growing self esteem journey.

"Certain friends" however, may feel jealous or envious that you are becoming more self assured and happier than they are. Human beings are used to familiarity and when they see something or someone change or reform people's reactions are different according to how they feel.

You are not faking or aping your way to higher self esteem; rather beneficial thoughts and behaviours are created within that personally serve you and are being projected out into your world.

The main thing that we must take into consideration here is that you are gaining higher self esteem so **you** can make **yourself** feel centred and more satisfied about **your** life.

<u>We do not make this a selfish act!</u>

We do it in a way that "we deserve for ourselves" and if you haven't been giving yourself the attention you deserve, this is a great time for you to start.

When you do something beneficial for your growth, especially something as big this, it will become part of your life forever. After this has happened, you won't be able to stop recalling the revelation that you have made. You will appreciate and respect yourself and this will greatly contribute to the wonderful feelings you experience each and every day.

A part of you may not want to change

There maybe a little feeling inside that's trying to stop you from creating the emotions and life experiences you truly desire.

Remember this deterring feeling only comes up because it's a self defence mechanism. Believe it or not some people are often afraid of their own success. We are so used to doing things in one way that when we begin to learn a new way that serves us, there's suddenly a part of our brains that go "wait a second, this is what I'm used to, why are we changing?"

<u>The ego is always resistant to what is truly best for you.</u>

This part of you is not against you, it was just so used to what you were used to that when you want to change for the better, the brain thinks it doesn't want to change; but you will change the more you put in effort towards WANTING to change.

<u>This cycle must be broken</u> as **you want to grow stronger**

When you continue affirming that you want to restyle, which you do; the feeling will fade into insignificance and a fruit will begin to grow in its place. Imagine this fruit to be of what your dreams are made up of.

This entire book is about learning to work in harmony with your feelings; so if a weary feeling ever does come up, it is only trying to tell you what is going on. Listen to this feeling if it comes up, make some new distinctions and then realize it's just an opportunity to learn; so become aware as something new and different is about to happen, something new and exciting that contributes to your future success.

A big part of you wants to change

There's a big part of you that wants to change. The part of you that imagines what it feels like when you experience an ever growing success.

This feeling can be so powerful that all you want to do is change right now!

Imagine what it's going to be like when you begin to feel a stronger sense of value from within?

WE ALL HAVE DREAMS and there is a place inside of you that imagines waking up tomorrow morning, possessing everything you have ever wanted. What if these feelings suddenly become locked within you forever?

Use this feeling to guide you because this feeling will serve you in becoming successful. Suck the juice out of what is filled with success and allow it to guide you in creating your new exciting life.

Dreams and goals are to be focused and worked towards, until they become your physical reality.

Pay attention carefully and you may recognize that this is what your inner self is trying to tell you: to gain the habit of living your life to create an effortless process of achievement.

You deserve to live your dreams! Follow the emotions your dreams bring up within you to move closer towards making them real.

You are worth more, to prove to yourself that YOU CAN SUCCEED **for you**.

In a nutshell

1. Changing for other people may not allow you to hold onto what you have gained

2. Your hesitation is a sign of what needs to be strengthened and learned from

3. There's a place inside of you that craves a fulfilling life, as you feel this run with it into the future

Using your conscious and unconscious

Your feelings are constantly asking you to direct them in what you consciously believe to be right from wrong.

When an emotion pops up, it is in response to what your focus and attention is placed upon. To put it simply; whatever you focus on, will generate a response that consists of thoughts, feelings and behaviours.

Imagine if a shy guy wants to approach his boss for a raise but whenever his boss walks by he feels stuck, he is only stuck due to the negative response he feels that deters him from following through in the moment he is in.

This negative emotion pops up in relation to his boss because the unconscious has been previously taught feelings of rejection in reaction to asking for a raise - and thus brings these feelings back up all over again automatically whenever the opportunity to demand more money passes by.

He then accidentally makes the conscious decision to affirm his nervousness by deciding not to take action because of the negative feelings he experiences. And this only teaches his unconscious that it's doing a good job because he doesn't correct the mistakes and instead, just runs with the entire negative process! And he wonders why he isn't earning what he's worth.

The unconscious is very subjective to what decisions and actions you take.

Never ignore your emotions, only use them to your advantage to become more of the person you are aiming to be.

Intercept

We must become aware of when disempowering feelings pop up in relation towards particular subjects, so we can begin to intercept them - to create new trains of thought that lead into empowering directions when the time comes. This will teach your unconscious the new directions that you, the authority, desires to obtain.

This is easy. All you need to do is consciously use your imagination in a way that makes you feel good. If nervous feelings where to pop up smell imaginary warm apply pie. Relax into a warm steamy Jacuzzi bubbling around you. Picture yourself experiencing the thrill of a bungee jump.

First **intercept**, then FEEL good and then cut off from negative feelings that you are no longer willing to put up with when they appear.

Consciously stick up for your unconscious and protect it from any external or internal negative feelings that **you** ultimately **do not** want. Your unconscious is after all a major part of who you are and adapts to who you **choose** to become in the near future.

Replace negative thoughts, with positive everything!

Direct

The conscious mind has the ability to take action despite disempowering emotions that come up. For example, if the "stuck" guy from earlier took action despite his nervous feelings, he could have discovered new empowering sensations and reasons for why asking for a raise wasn't such a big deal after all.

This proves that you have the conscious ability to direct and completely drive yourself to success, regardless of any emotion that stands in your way!

Taking action despite the negative emotions you experience will allow you and your unconscious to learn VERY QUICKLY. As long as you use your focus and behaviours in uplifting directions that permits you to learn more.

Feelings are not even necessarily real, they are just memories and processes stored and ran by your unconscious, only seeming real due to the feelings that accompany them, to which you can choose to work through them by consciously supporting yourself DESPITE how it feels.

Exercise

Would you protect a child from harm?

Since your unconscious is like your own child, you must protect it from harm and teach it to grow.

1. Think of a child you would do anything to protect or think of yourself as when you were a child

2. Now imagine the innocence of this child that you want to protect from harm becomes a part of your emotional system

3. From now on do whatever it takes to protect your inner child from harm and lead by example of what you want your child to learn

Would you ever abandon a child you are responsible for?

In a nutshell

1. Intercept unwanted emotions and redirect them into directions that serve

2. Use your conscious decisions and actions to create the habits you aspire to right **now** in THIS moment

3. Protect your inner child (your unconscious) from unwanted influences and never abandon yourself ever again!

Will

What determines your results?

The ultimate power in being able to exercise your will.

Now, some people will refer to will as 'will power' but the word "power" attached to the end of the word will only confuses us when it comes to really understanding what our will truly is.

Most of us think of power as strength, position of authority or control

The word power added to the end of our own will, speaks in terms of effort or an ability that is used, possessed or has been gained.

But this doesn't help us to understand anything!

We understand that somebody can have the ability to do a cartwheel, or a speaker having the ability to produce sounds, or the human eye possessing the ability to see. But to speak of the ability to will, leaves us completely confused to understand how naturally EFFORTLESS our will really is.

Will: **To make a reasoned choice, decision and action**

In other words, force and effort is not required when using will. As will is being able to choose, decide and act.

We have the will to do so, as we have the **freedom of choice**. However, this does not mean we can do whatever we want.

You cannot make someone do something against their own will

A person 'could' make someone take action by making them feel scared or excited enough. But that someone **chooses** and acts based on their own decisions.

A person that is scared chooses to succumb to fear by their own decisions. Someone that is excited enough decides to act according to their own reasons.

You cannot make someone do something against their own reasons and decisions, because they reason and decide according to what they choose is best for them.

The notion of somebody making someone do something against their will - is ridiculous. When you tell someone to jump they don't automatically do it every time unless they have a reason or have chosen to do so.
We all possess the ability to will and this must not be mistaken with "will power", which means to apply effort to make a simple decision.

It doesn't take any effort to use your will. It's just a case of deciding to move your muscles and directing your focus in the directions you want.

Everybody has will - and for the person that has the typical "will power" label, is just someone that has become used to making decisions, and then acting upon them; as a result, they have unleashed the natural power we all possess within us.

The so called 'strongest will powered person in the world' has no power of will over you, as we all have the same ability to choose, decide, think and move alike. THE POINT HERE IS THAT WE ARE ALL USING THE SAME ABILITY!

Will is just a case of: Will you? Or Wont you?

If you will do something; then you will use your will to take action.

Trying to use power or force against your own ability to decide and act is pointless, because you'll only be resisting against your natural ability of body and mind.

When you can't be bothered to do something, you are really implying that you can't be bothered to move your own body.

If you end up fighting against yourself to take action, relax and start again - to gain the habit of being able to use your will naturally and effortlessly.

Above all, the choices and decisions you make in the **present** regarding your unbeneficial thoughts and behaviours that you are aware of, are completely your choice if you continue to persist in them. In other words, if you become aware of your negative thoughts or behaviours and continue to do them, that's your own choice.

Are you going to choose a direction that serves you or not?

If you do not make empowering, beneficial decisions in how you want to live your life; then you have already made a decision haven't you?

You have made the decision to be directed and controlled by your environment instead of creating the future you deserve.

Make decisions that benefit your life's higher self esteem.

Determination is directed focus and action, and action is what impacts your daily life.

<u>Act upon your beneficial feelings and decisions. And use effortless will in life</u> to reach the given end of your desired goals.

In a nutshell

1. Will "power" is described as effort and this is WRONG!

2. To will - is to make choices, decide and act

3. Get used to using your will until it naturally becomes effortless

5. Will you - or wont you?

Failure Is Not Failure

What prevents people from chasing after their dreams?

The answer is: **Fear of failure!**

The word failure for most people means something they are not good at, unable to achieve or something that doesn't work when they try to use or do something.

Some of us take up new business ventures or try to learn a new language, only to have it not work out the way how we planned it to. In this case we are quick to throw in the towel and class it as a 'failure'.

However, when something doesn't work, it doesn't mean we should give up!

When you were a baby learning how to walk, the first few attempts you fell on your bottom. If when you were a baby you decided to give up on walking; you just went "screw this I'm a failure it doesn't work!" You wouldn't be able to walk today.

Nobody can really be a 'failure' because all it takes is using your body to try again, and again, and again in moving towards the pursuit of your dreams. Just like when you were a baby, you naturally learned from your mistakes and used a different approach every time until you succeeded.

Therefore the principle of 'failure' is only true when a person decides to change their decision to **not** pursue their goals. To put it simply; they make a new decision, a decision to give up!

Failure is NOT a disease automatically inherited when things don't work out when we try.

So **if** something doesn't work understand that you are learning and developing as a person, only to help you succeed even more!

If I personally gave up in the pursuit of gaining my own higher self esteem, I would probably be dead! I realized that I must not give up on myself and kept pushing to be the best person I have always dreamed to be, and I still continue to do so.

Apply these beneficial principles to the frustrations, stresses and mishaps that happen in your own life and you **will** always find the way.

Those who are NOT successful only want things to work out right all the time and give up when things don't. **You are** required to make mistakes and learn from them; otherwise you wouldn't know the difference between what works and what doesn't work in your life.

This is the only way how you will improve for the better! And if these new thoughts and actions you have come up with didn't work, figure out some better ideas that do work, and continue to try again and again until you reach your desired result.

To become successful you must fail more than you **ever have before** by taking action consistently and always learning from your mistakes.

Failure is feedback and is the foundation of life success!

People that ARE currently successful radiate success because they fail more times than anybody else. And if **it is** the continuous process of dusting themselves off to take more shots at their targets, is what keeps them moving in the right directions, YOU should **do** the same!

If you ever run into a dead end build new bridges by asking yourself: How precisely did I do that? What exactly did I do that didn't work? When did I do this? Is timing important? Where did I do this? Is the location noteworthy here?

Become wiser by making a few distinctions that will allow you to increase your intelligence - personally changing yourself into an individual that easily creates life success.

Never change your decisions, only become progressively witty, perceptive and elegant in your approach and you will naturally always find the way.

Use your will to continuously take action!

You can leave everyone else to think of 'failure' as a silly disease and you can convince yourself that YOU CREATE YOUR OWN DESTINY; and will learn to become even more productive and capable along the way.

Set out to fail and then succeed in life because this way you'll always learn something new. Become curious about your 'failures' and use them to guide your future actions to produce subsequent results.

In a nutshell

1. A person has only failed when they choose to make the decision to give up

2. Setbacks and mistakes are the learning's in life that allow you to grow. Take any action you see fit and adapt towards the achievements of your goals, no matter how uncomfortable it may seem at first

3. Open **yourself** up to the new learning's that life offers and keep using your will to take action

Taking Time for You

Taking time for you is very important. As when you do this, you can come up with new ideas on how to make things even better than the wonderful learning's you have already discovered. This is what spending time for you offers.

There are many things that stop us from taking time for ourselves. These include:

> The stresses of life: Meaning the things we have to do on a daily basis, like paying the bills, doing laundry or going to work.
>
> And the stress of attending to other people's needs and wants.

The general tasks we go through in our daily lives **have to** be done. We have been doing them for sometime now and have become quite good at them. The only problem is that people base their whole lives on these everyday problems. We've been dealing with petty disputes from the ages of 7; don't you think its now time to be above it all?

Little things may come along and get in the way, and this is fine since it's a sign of life and we can learn from everyday problems. But when you realize that you **don't** have to spend less time for yourself, just because of your environment; You will be led into a place where you can make your life feel even better, despite the daily tasks that have to be done and even better than that, while you're executing those daily tasks.

The things we have to do

Some people may feel as if they don't have any freedom in their lives; they let their external circumstances bring them down. They may feel trapped and restricted because of the demands on their time or having to put up with the stresses of others.

We tend to whine or think about things like "I hate paying my bills!" "Why do I have to do this why can't somebody else do it?" "Why cant you just get off my case, everybody is driving me mad!" "I need to make it on time or I'll be late!" (Even though you have plenty of time as it is) "First of all, I've got to do this, then I must to do this, then I have to do that…"

Normal everyday problems and challenges shouldn't have degrading emotions attached to them; otherwise we'll feel this way everyday we live through them. This will only clutter our heads with unnecessary thoughts which **are not good for anything.**

Don't get wrapped up and stressed over the things that are wrong with your life now, what may happen in the future and what happened a while ago. **Instead**, focus on how to make things fun, manageable and even better as you go through the daily motions of living.

Become perceptive towards complaining or blaming and only practice to become more efficient in those areas of life you need to.

Everything you experience during your journey into higher self esteem, whether pleasant or unpleasant happens for a reason and a purpose that serves you.

Consider the fact that everything you have been through in your life, and still going through now, leads up to your destiny towards life success, gradually learning along the way.

Grow with creating the life you want within and gain a sense of seeing the outside world through new eyes.

Inside and then out

When you build a stronger foundation of success within yourself first, you will begin to contribute workable approaches to dealing with situations in your life in a way you really want to.

Imagine if you were contributing ideas to a success team you were a part of. If you don't have anything practical within yourself to contribute to the team, your participation is practically worthless.

This principle is the same when gaining anything in life!

Imagine what it's like when you project faith and certainty towards achieving your goals. You will always have the positive feelings within yourself first, so whatever life throws at you, you can always fall back on your faith and certainty, because you have someone to encourage and comfort you. **YOU!**

You must create a basis for what you want, and what you truly deserve for yourself. This will allow you to project your **inner** self esteem out into the external world easily and protectively.

Whatever frustrations or setbacks get in your way you can always refer back to the empowering feelings you have already created within.

Spend time with yourself to figure out new ways in how you can feel good when dealing with stress, connecting with others, strengthening your inner worth and overall success in all the areas of life you can muster.

Manage yourself in directions that benefit you so you can **learn** to become on top of things.

Go out and walk the dog as a means to get some exercise for your legs, make that important phone call now, so you can get some relaxation time later-on during the day. And do the cooking for the family according to what you want to eat. Always put yourself first in a humble way and confidence will spread like wildfire everywhere you go.

If a stronger inner sense of motivation will enable you to connect with your dreams, strengthen motivation within you. And learn through trial an error to perceive your external world based on what you are creating within.

When you squeeze an orange the juice that comes out consists of what's inside. If someone squeezes you and out comes happiness, motivation, fulfilment and success, it will spill out into every area of your life.

Create from within the inside first, and use these new positive feelings to adapt them towards your environment in a way that signifies higher self esteem and more...!

In a nutshell

1. Don't let the tasks you do on a daily basis prevent you from becoming more of who you deserve to be

2. Spend time with yourself to contemplate in ways you can make life more manageable and easier for yourself.

3. Discover in the new beneficial thoughts that you can manifest within yourself and use them to prevent daily stress to create a happier life

Your unconscious - Your Friend

For the most part the only reason why we do not feel wonderful everyday by following a road to success is because the conscious and unconscious minds are in certain disagreement. Meaning the thoughts you consciously want hasn't yet been accepted by the unconscious or whatever the unconscious brings up in response you may not consciously want to experience. To release yourself from your mind you must be **in** co-operation with yourself.

The process in you discovering and getting to know your unconscious is a very uplifting experience and is almost like becoming best friends with yourself all over again. When you come to terms with the realism in your life, whether it being what you physically do or the thoughts and feelings you generally have; you will grow in a much deeper understanding of getting to know yourself better.

Name your unconscious

To become closer to your unconscious you need to have a name for it.

Names make us feel connected to people, places and objects.

Imagine if you spent a whole week with a stranger trying to get to know them without ever knowing their name; i'm guessing after that week you may still feel slightly uncomfortable with them.

How would you call them from across the room? How would you introduce them to a friend? How would you gain their attention to ask important questions?

There would be somewhat of a mystery there as to whom this person really is. It's the same notion of you missing out on the natural connection you have with your own unconscious.

To become reacquainted with your unconscious you must come up with a name for it. Once you name your unconscious you will immediately feel re-connected and can discover what you're **really** like.

You can if you want to use your middle name, or a made up name that makes sense to you. You can even use the name of your favourite superhero (if you have one). But be sure to come up with a name that doesn't make you feel a sense of separateness from your unconscious.

You can try asking your unconscious for the name it wants and then notice if any name pops into mind that makes sense to you.

Naming your unconscious will develop a connection in you being able to communicate and discover what it has learnt, and will also allow you to teach it better.

Take some time to **think of a name right now**...

And finally be happy that you and your unconscious are now friends and both want to help each other in creating the feelings and life experiences you deserve.

Unconscious discovery

1. Find a quite place where you can relax

2. Close your eyes

3. Playfully challenge your unconscious to dig up an uplifting memory you wish to remember

4. Say "Ok.... (Unconscious)....bring up.... (Then choose the memory you want). Challenge your unconscious to bring up the positive memory as fast and in as much clarity as possible

Your unconscious favourite memories

1. Follow steps 1-4 from "unconscious discovery" but this time; ask your unconscious to bring up its favourite memories.

You will notice pleasant memories being recalled back to you. And if you consciously like these memories, why not thank your unconscious that you acknowledge and appreciate them.

Problem areas

(Read this once before you do it for the first time)

Your unconscious speaks in terms of symbols, meaning it responds to you with certain visual representations according to what you are asking about. With this exercise you can become aware of problem areas and take a shot at figuring out how your unconscious has interpreted them.

1. Close your eyes for a minute and think of a negative problem area in your life

2. Ask your unconscious to give you a symbol to what you are asking about

E.g. you may ask about some motivational weaknesses, and your unconscious may respond by bringing up an image of a garden without any plants.

3. Whatever image, feeling or symbol comes up that is held by your unconscious; you can analyze and discover how this may be preventing your personal growth, and discover some alternative ways in how you want to feel instead

If an image doesn't appear at first - try again.

4. Whatever does come up: realize it is only a learned response from the unconscious. These symbols are not predictive or real, they are just processes once learned that you are discovering in and reforming for the better.

(Soon after you have begun to come to terms with you unconscious, it will begin to open up to you. Almost as if you know exactly how you feel and think about things because you have previously asked your unconscious about it.

You will get to know yourself better by establishing powerful links to positive subjects held within the depths of your mind.)

PART THREE

DEPROGRAMMING NEGATIVE PATTERNS AND HABITS

Negative Internal Dialogue

The dialogue we use in our heads to think in our daily lives hugely affect us.

The one voice that continuously goes through your head every minute of the day is your own, and you abide by this voice before anyone else's.

At times we can use our own self talk in a way that is limiting to our success.

For example: What do you tell yourself when you are about to try something new? Do you say "I can never do this" Or do you say "This will be easy for me!"

We pretty much talk ourselves into things and this results in how we feel - leading onto what actions we take in the future.

Your identity

Talking negatively towards our own identity is like a phoney self admittance.

'I' - is frequently used in statements like these since we are addressing ourselves, and then giving a suggestion of what we think we are.

These statements usually go like this:

"I am worthless"
"I can't do it!"
"I am incapable"
"I knew I was a failure"
"I feel like crap"

These statements are opinions of what you think you are. The only reason why you think you are is because certain emotions accompany it.

So we actually recall our memories before we can say "Oh yeah, I forgot, I'm worthless".

Stop attempting to be less by hanging onto your past and begin to start becoming more of who you want to be by alternating to something else that is positive.

Talking negative to yourself

People talk to themselves in an authoritative manner, almost as if they are a commander telling themselves what to do.

Imagine if you joined the army, having to put up with a sergeant screaming offensive downgrading comments at you. Using words like "You can't" "You don't" "You wasn't" - all the while spitting in your face trying to bear the stench of his unbearable breath.

This is what we create when we use the negative authoritive voice in our own heads. We somewhat attack ourselves in terms of the 2nd person.

And it's pretty tuff when people think they should put up with their own downgrading dialog because this generally stunts our self success and encouragement.

So for this example I'll choose to verbally abuse myself.

"You cannot do it nick!"
"Nick, you were always worthless!"
"You are not going to succeed!"
"Don't do it Nick!"
"Hey Nick, You suck!"

These statements are all used against me, by me!

If I did this for a whole week about my weaknesses and the things I am really trying hard to create, you can be pretty sure I'll feel down in the dumps about achieving them.

Make sure whenever you catch yourself using this self talk - learn to encourage and push yourself in the right directions towards success.

In the now

People occasionally acknowledge everything that is terrible in life and put themselves down about it because they think it can't be changed.

This type of 'bewildering' self dialog, makes people focus on all the things that aren't right with their lives, rather than appreciating what they currently have and want to create.

This type of dialog is generally used in the following:

"This is rubbish"
"Things can't get any worse"
"My life sucks"
"This is hard"

If you had a parrot on your shoulder constantly reminding you of all the flaws in your life, you would eventually get fed up and stuff its beak with crackers: and maybe its time for you to do the same thing with your own negative dialogue.

Stop attacking your identity by giving yourself silly opinions based on past experiences and external events that you are trying your best to deal with in your very own way.

Questions about the negative

Questions initiate thinking. Whenever you ask yourself a question, your mind **almost always** comes up with an answer.

What did you eat for breakfast? Did you take a shower this morning?

These questions; when asked to yourself, surface answers.

Try not to answer this question I'm about to ask you: How old are you?

Now, you most likely answered that question in your head even if you didn't want to. If you didn't answer the question; can you remember how old you are?

The problem with questions when not used properly is they can make us feel very degrading states.

For example:

"Why does this always have to happen to me?"
"Why am I so worthless?"
"Why can't I do anything right"
"Why do I always fail?"

These questions will bring up negative answers **most of the time**, and usually leave us feeling even worse.

When someone asks themselves the question "Why am I so incapable?" the brain usually responds, so the answer to that questions would probably be "because you're a moron!" Ask a lousy question, and you will most likely receive a lousy answer that doesn't make you feel good at all.

If you were to ask "What can I do to become stronger?" a different set of answers will pop up that you can ACTUALLY use.

Ask BETTER questions and you'll most likely receive a BETTER answer.

Belittling dialog

Have you ever achieved something that was worth praising yourself about, but then brushed it aside like it never happened?

We sometimes use our self talk in a way that belittles our accomplishments. Almost as if we get muddled up between what is supposed to be praised, as opposed to what needs paying hardly any attention at all.

We use this dialog in the following:

"Oh, it was nothing"
"It was bound to happen sooner or later"
"I was lucky"
"All by the roll of the dice"
"No big deal"

This is an act of failing to acknowledge oneself.

What's it like when you do recognize the struggles and great mountains you've climbed - only having to reach the top, listening to someone say to you "So what, I could've done that with no hands, you ain't nothing!"

Choosing to use belittling dialog will not only wipe out the compliments of your achievements but also the wonderful feelings that come along with it.

WHERE EXACLY DO WE GET THIS STUFF FROM ANYWAY?! DON'T DO IT TO YOURSELF!

Always acknowledge your past success and if you ever find yourself in the process of achieving, grab hold of every self compliment you can think of and never let go! Let it be a reminder of what you are **truly** capable of in the future, and use these new feelings to press on.

Exercise

This exercise is used to talk yourself out of any disempowering reasoning or negative emotions.

1. Think of some negative dialog that you use that holds you back

2. Hold this thought - and say: "Looking back, up until now, it was silly for me to act in that way".

3. Now say "Realizing this, as I look forward, I can effortlessly make the beneficial choices now, to focus on what I desire"

4. And now focus on the new positive feelings you want

Note: You can also vary certain key words in this, for example: You, This, I, behave, think, feel in terms of what you are referring to.

E.g. "Looking back, up until now, it was silly to even think in that way"

"Realizing this, as you look forward, you can effortlessly make the choice now, to focus on what you desire"

Mix and match to find out which key words work best for you.

Disempowering internal dialog comes in forms of:

You are.... (Authoritative negative attack)

I am.... (Phoney self admittance)

This is.... (Putting everything down)

Why....? (A disempowering question)

Ah well.... (And belittling personal achievements)

In a nutshell

1. Start becoming aware of how you talk to yourself when it concerns your capability, self worth and future

2. List some of the disempowering internal dialog you have used in the past, to help you spot these little critters if they pop up again

3. Whenever you recognize negative dialog in the moment, stop yourself to purposely use the positive opposite instead whether true or not. E.g. "I am worthless = "I am Brilliant"

Remember: You talk yourself into feeling and doing things, since you don't listen to anybody else's voice more than your own. **Be careful what you are talking yourself into!**

Negative Images and Movies Are Your Playthings

Everybody has the ability to visualize. To prove this to yourself, answer the following questions:

What colour is the sky? What do the clouds look like? What colour are they?

Do you maybe, see a picture in your mind? These images may not be completely clear, but as you imagine, you gain a sense of what you remember and see without being directly in front of it.

Going into your imagination allows you to experience certain feelings. Your mind doesn't know the difference between something you vividly imagine as opposed to what you actually experience.

For example: Stop for a moment to visualize the last time you were in front of your favourite food! Maybe it's a chocolate cake, your mouth watering - waiting to take that first bite of pleasure.

Now, imagine the delicious chocolate cake again; but this time notice there is a hundred slimy maggots all over it, worming their way in and out of the chocolaty centre.

How do you feel about eating this chocolate cake now?

Guessing you felt the accompanied emotions as you used your imagination. It is no mistake that whatever pictures you make in your mind has an effect on **how** you feel about what you want.

Occasionally some people just haven't seemed to get that negative memory out of their heads, due to the reasons and feelings that they had towards it.

It could be a mental image of a time where they felt really low of themselves, or a scenario of them doing something wrong over and over again.

You can alter negative images and movies to take the emotional charge out of mental impressions and since the mind learns, you will learn these new feelings associated to what you want.

Exercise

1. Recall a very unpleasant memory or situation that has a negative effect on you today

2. Now physically point to where ever this unpleasant memory **seems** to be coming from. Notice if it is a movie or still image, does it have colour? How big is it?

3. Freeze the memory and sense it becoming black and white; rapidly rewind it and forward it from beginning to end and see it gradually turn fuzzy, and watch the image shrink in size - rewind and forward it even faster now and visualize the image going far back and disappearing into the distance.

You can also make certain people in the image look funny by changing them into funny cartoon characters by doing this exercise all over again. Make the person that annoys you grow a funny clown nose and give them Mickey Mouse ears. Notice you can feel even better about the situation than ever before.

Shredder exercise

(Take time to learn this exercise before you do it)

If you had a shredder what would it look like?

If you had a blender what would it look like?

1. Recall a negative memory you would like to feel better about, preferably the first time it happened or when the pain felt most terrible

2. Notice and point to where you sense it coming from

3. Now put the memory into the shredder you created earlier ready to go in: You will see the negative memory being shredded, coming out the other end in strips of film or paper.

4. Grab these strips and put them into the blender (you created earlier) and watch the blender cutting it into fine pieces of paper or film.

5. Sprinkle these fine little pieces out and watch them being blown away forever into the wind.

Internal Negative Voices Are Your Playthings

Critical internal voices and even unpleasant sounds that people hear within their minds affect them drastically.

And changing the context of what these voices and sounds are put in, will change how we feel about them.

Let's try a little experiment:

Stop for a moment and think of a person that you remember how their voice sounds, and hear them say "You're worthless".

Now change their voice to a high pitch squeaky voice saying "You're worthless". Now allow it to drop in bass, to become a slow paced dopey voice "you're worthless". Now change into a loving sexy voice and hear them say "you're worthless"

You will notice the feelings produced by the original statement have changed!

But take note that these are the voices you hear 'inside' of your mind NOT the voice that you consciously refer to as "me"!

Can you remember a time when you couldn't get an argument out of your head? You may have incoherently played the negative voice over and over again during moments of the day, which only made you feel worse.

You can easily change the affects of any **internal negative** voice you hear inside of your head by changing the tonality, pitch, tempo and volume of it.

In effect, when you make these voices sound squeaky, dopey, fast, passionate etc...You automatically **change** the feelings brought about by them.

DJ exercise

Read through this before you do it

1. Close your eyes and recall a person (or your own) negative criticising voice

2. Notice where it is coming from - and imagine this place being a speaker

3. Now visualize an equalizer in front of you as if you were a DJ. (An equalizer the gadget with many knobs and dials that can alter the effect of an original sound)

4. Put the negative criticising voice to play on repeat and hear it coming from the speaker, fiddle with the knobs on the equalizer to change the pitch, volume, speed, rhythm, tonality etc. Play with it to make the voice sound funny and amusing until you burst out laughing at it!

Above all, have fun!

Body

Our behaviours affect the way how we feel.

Dancing allows us to experience different emotions as opposed to when we are just sitting down. This is because the mind and body are connected.

Can you remember the last time you felt upset about something? Your body was probably in a slump which only made you feel worse. Or what about those times when you feel really lazy - not being bothered to move your own body.

You can interrupt negative emotions by using your body **differently**!

The more you interrupt those negative emotions with full out moving and behavioural engagement; you can instantly change your emotions right now.

Can you remember a time when you were having a conversation with someone that got interrupted? You may have lost your train of thought for a moment - finding it difficult to get back to what you were saying.

This principle is the same when using your body to interrupt negative emotional states.

Recall a time when you felt really low and as you feel these feelings, physically do an outrageous crazy and silly dance that represents you are having fun! This will interrupt the negative pattern immediately.

Just like when you are reminded of a time when you heard something funny. And as it is recalled you cut off from old emotions - and instantly experience new positive behaviours in its place.

Think of some behaviours that allow you to feel happy and empowered. You may impersonate someone from a TV show or a movie you like or you can use funny comments and gestures, it's up to you. Do whatever feels good to counteract unpleasant situations.

Exercise

1. Bring any horrible emotion up to the surface and allow yourself to experience it

2. As you are feeling this emotion, immediately interrupt it by doing a crazy and outrageous movement. Make your behaviour explosive and completely insane to make yourself feel better

Breathing

Breathing is the constant sign that reminds us we are alive. Breathing allows our bodies to intake oxygen and carries it through our blood cells. If we do not breathe we die!

Since breathing is an important aspect of our life, regulating it will change how we feel.

When a person panics their breathing increases due to what is focused on when their breathing is slowed down however, they begin to relax and feel calmer.

When you instantly regulate your breathing right now, feelings will change as breathing can be played with.

Let's try a little experiment:

Purposely breathe franticly as if you are panicking and out of breath...

Now slow down your breathing pace and take long, deep and relaxing breaths...

When you feel relaxing sensations you are automatically compelled to breathe out a big "aahhh" as you relax into this moment right now.

Breathing effects the way how you feel and is a symbol of life!

Breath exercise

(Read through this once before you do it for the first time)

1. Imagine what positive feelings you would like to experience, maybe a desired future experience or a pleasant experience from the past

2. Sit or lie down and get comfortable. your eyes can be opened or closed

3. Take in a nice deep and full breath

4. Hold in for 4 seconds while thinking about this positive experience

5. Now exhale your breath until you reach the end

6. Now hold in again for another 4 seconds, while thinking about your positive experience

7. Now breathe in again.

Repeat this cycle for up to 4 times to gain a relaxed stress-free state of wonder. While you hold your breath you shouldn't be counting, only using your imagination. (Use your intuition to judge what 4 seconds mean to you)

Your Emotional Body Field

Emotions are experienced all throughout your body in different places. Confidence is a completely different emotion to sadness. It is experienced differently in terms of how and where it is felt within you.

When you imagine what it is like to experience feelings of total confidence, where do you feel those feelings coming from first? Where do they go next?

Now remember a time when you felt a feeling of sadness, where do you feel those feelings coming from first? Where does it go to next?

When you **remember** where success preventing emotions come from, you can learn to discard them and cancel them out.

Emotions do have labels but for the most part they are just different processes. Remember, the unconscious does not know the difference between what is good or not, this means you can attach different meanings to different emotions.

Imagine if when a belittling feeling pops up - you are able to delete it instantly. Like an alien with a zapper gun, zapping those disempowering feelings into dust.

After you have denied, deleted and eliminated negative feelings time after time, they won't be coming back any longer because you have learned DIFFERENTLY!

Call up negative feelings one by one and say:

"Due to your non beneficial work ethic your stupidity in not giving to me what this company needs, you are now fired from the job!"

Notice the useless emotion sob off into the distance.

The vortex

You can use this technique anytime you wish to suck the power out of those negative emotions you don't want.

The vortex is like a whirlpool. This whirlpool turns anti-clockwise as it draws the negative feelings inside, like water going down a plug hole.

The whirlpool generates positive emotions; these positive feelings can be associated with a colour of your liking.

Experiment with some positive emotions you can attach a colour to - forming your positive vortex; imagine it spinning inside drawing positive feelings back and down into oblivion.

Exercise

1. Purposely bring up a negative feeling

2. Notice where the negative feeling is coming from

3. Imagine your positive vortex placed behind it spinning anti-clockwise - drawing the negative emotion into the whirlpool of positive oblivion

You should feel the negative emotion diminish and lose its power.

This exercise can be done whenever a negative feeling occurs to rectify the problem or can be done purposely to weaken negative feelings you didn't want.

Get used to using the vortex - it will easily get rid of any anxiety or nervousness.

The zapper

This exercise will enable you to instantly delete any negative feeling in a different way.

Imagine inside there is a space aged gun that can zap disempowering feelings away.

1. Now notice where the negative emotions is coming from

2. Imagine a flash of laser beam (of a colour that feels good) instantly zapping and deleting the negative feelings into nothingness. You may see dust or tiny pieces of disintegrated sparkles

You can use this zapping exercise whenever a negative feeling comes up. You can also destroy negative feelings purposely by bringing them up, and zapping them away.

How Negative Feelings Are Formed

Your self defence is being able to stick up for yourself, you do not allow negative outside influences to affect your life in any way. Decide to go on a negativity 'fast' and focus only on empowering feelings from now on.

If when a person ever accidentally accepts negative influences, their first protective stage is broken.

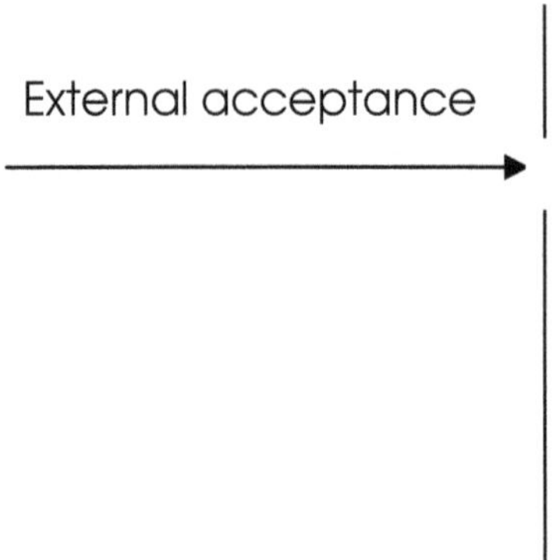

When we keep our guards up, and do not accept external negativity the diagram will look like this.

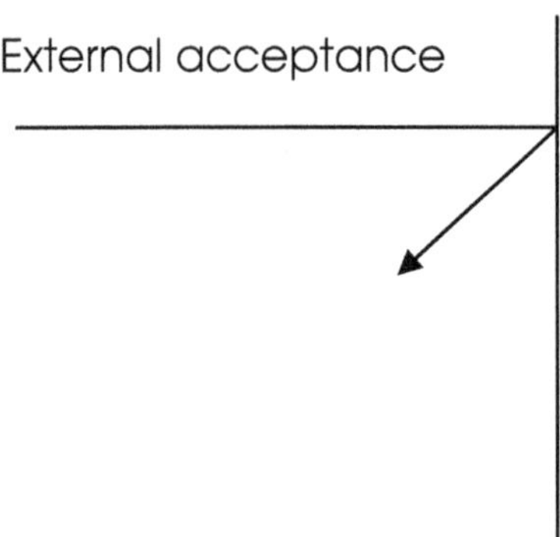

Declining negative external influences will allow you to keep your self assurance and respect intact as you protect your **self** and do NOT let anyone affect your higher self esteem.

Reason or reconsider the outside influences in anyway you can, to turn it to your benefit. NEVER just do nothing! Even **'trying'** to protect yourself will allow you to learn and grow in becoming stronger - and a protective barrier will slowly begin to form.

Reject negative outside influences from now on.

Below are the three stages in which low self esteem or any other self defeating emotion is created.

Stage one

If external influences are accidentally accepted in the moment we 'trip up' onto stage one. And this is the start of internal negative thinking.

Negative thinking can be about anything that is attacking the self; whether putting ourselves down about our self esteem, confidence, capability, current circumstance...etc.

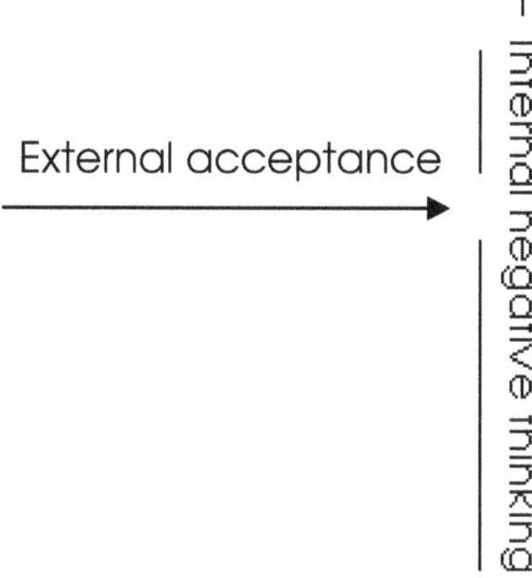

Attacking of the self may arise from own personal negative thought processes or can be triggered by an external influence.

In terms of external we may have been put down by someone and decided to attack our own worth, all because we considered if what they said was true.

Negative internal thinking can start by acknowledging our own errors; we may have attacked ourselves for them instead of using it to become stronger - to turn it into something beneficial and empowering.

Whether if disempowering thinking comes about by external or internal, it affects us because these thoughts are built upon images, sounds, internal dialogue, behaviours and emotions. So make sure you use the tools you have learned up until now to get rid of them, whenever you have the opportunity to become aware of yourself.

Stage two

If ever a person fuels negative thoughts and feelings this can lead onto them considering "whether if these thoughts and feelings are a part of whom they are" and this is stage two.

They in a sense stray away from their supposed beliefs and ponder on subjects that don't serve, by either chastising themselves or coming up with self defeating conclusions, based on the original thoughts from stage one.

They move on from what was first only an assumption to it being considered a part of their identity.

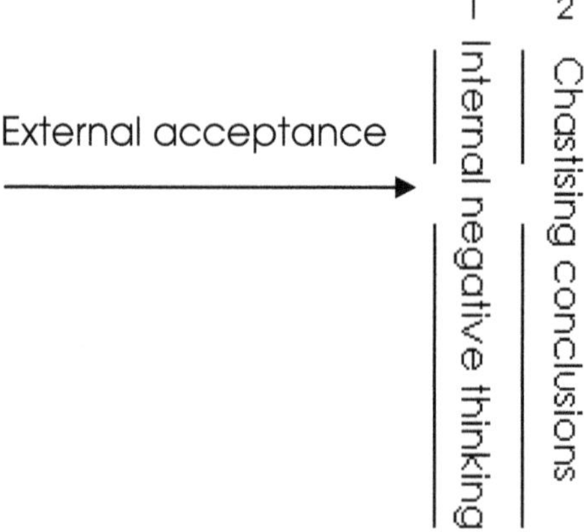

This is where the transition takes place between stage one and upcoming stage three - in-between the lines of being free or getting trapped. Don't make the mistake in being led to believe that you can't become a new higher levelled self esteemed person.

Notice what you are doing if you end up in this transition stage and turn it around for the better.

Life is an opportunity to become more abundant and you will do well to know this in times of doubt. RECONSIDER any seeds of doubt and use this stage to refer back to the uplifting emotions you were creating before.

If a person is not aware of when they should pull the plug on chastising conclusions, they can accidentally move onto...

Stage three

After stage two, comes stage three. This is where people eventually come up with overall opinions and beliefs about themselves that are so strong - that they behave in a way that affirms it.

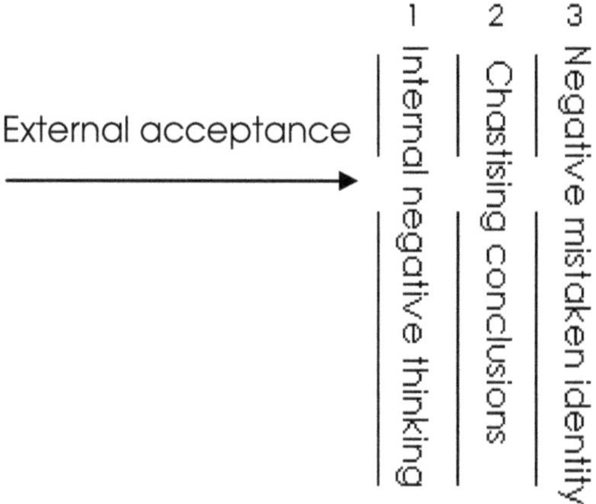

At stage three, negative mistaken identities are accidentally perceived by these people and only grow stronger if they stew what they ultimately do not want.

Remember, these identities are only perceived by the unconscious and are not even necessarily true. The only reason why they believe it to be true is because of the heavy baggage attached to self sabotaging ideas.

The main issue here is if we would've protected ourselves from stages 1 and 2 to begin with, these ideas wouldn't be real because we would have chosen **not** to learn them.

If you ever consider yourself in this stage crawl out of that hole until your fingers fall off AND NEVER LOOK BACK!

The loop

The final stage is what I like to call the loop. The loop begins after stage three because if we perceive our external reality in a self sabotaging way, this tends to start stage ones negative thinking all over again.

The looping of negativity will continue to go round and round until the pattern is broken.

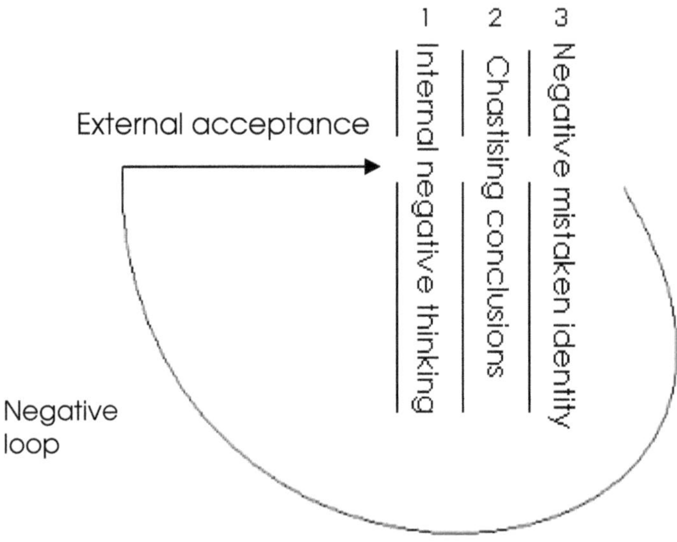

Continuously accepting negativity from stages one to three IS the road way to self destruction **and I have just laid it out for you.**

This loop can be broken at any stage when you become aware of what stage you're at. You can suddenly realize when it is happening and giggle in recognition "what am I doing?!" and then undermine and stop the negative pattern. And begin to utilize new alternative patterns from your new collection of skills.

Summary

Stage one: The beginning of external and internal negative influences

Stage two: Considering and/or chastising about thoughts and capabilities

Stage three: The attacking of the self, forming negative self identities and perceiving the external world in a disempowering way

In a nutshell

1. Do not allow negative feelings to get in or continue; whether it being from internal or external

2. Be attentive to any disempowering thoughts, feelings or behaviours and ALWAYS REFORM NEGATIVE LOOPS TO YOUR BENEFIT!

Say to yourself "You know what I can't be bothered to do this anymore, I quit!" and just relaxingly let it all go.

Wrap up

People seem to think that negative experiences are a big put down in life but I don't believe this to be true at all. The only time when these experiences are not serving you, is when you are not doing anything to use and learn from them.

We learn during tough times and struggles and these learning's will serve us in becoming more than we have ever dreamed possible.

Negative experiences are a blessing in our lives as they help us to learn and grow. If everything were easy, how would you know what inner strength and higher self esteem really is? So use this moment as a reminder for why you have already made the decisions to move towards your goals in an easy and peaceful way.

Using your will and learning from failure **will** create higher self esteem!

PART FOUR

USING POSITIVE PATTERNS AND HABITS EFFECTIVELY

You Do Want Positive Emotions

What's so great about strong positive uplifting emotions?

Positive emotions are ever growing and do not have any limits to them. They grow as you grow and eventually become embodied by you. And these new feelings will show up in every area of your life.

If this is not an amazing gift of life, I don't know what is. All we have to do to harness this power is **decide to** THINK IN THESE POSITIVE DIRECTIONS!

During the phase of listing all the qualities we enjoy about ANYTHING only makes us like these things even more as new reasons and associations are made in relation to them. And the more this is fuelled the more they expand - having a greater impact in our daily lives.

"*I don't know about you"*, but I'm beginning to wonder why I EVER felt discouraged about my own capability, self worth and possible life experiences in the **first place**!"

It's all about having the capacity to never give up in searching for the resources and doing whatever it takes to succeed.

All we need to do is become aware of what we have accomplished in our lives and apply the right feelings, attitudes, beliefs and actions to ourselves in a way that makes sense to us. So we can become even more successful than our biggest fans.

Will yourself to create and discover your dreams as being real inside of you today in a way that makes you feel good, about growing to become an inventor - of new empowering daily habits.

In a nutshell

1. Positive emotions are ever growing as they stack, multiply and compound on top of each other. When you discover in empowering possibilities, you naturally grow with them

2. Remember that the possibilities are literally endless when you dare to dream. Take those new next steps into higher levels of personal growth

Owning Your Positive Habitual and Conscious Emotions

To own your positive experiences you must acknowledge that you can make yourself feel good.

This can be done whenever you create uplifting moments for yourself or whenever your mind brings up beneficial responses automatically.

You will find yourself consciously feeling good in the moment as you do this exercise and will allow you to create upcoming success as to fully being the successful person you want to be.

The steps taken to **own** any empowering feeling that springs up are as follows: To first be grateful - then to embrace these feelings - and then to be thankful for the experience you've just created. This may sound simple, but these three emotions are actually very powerful positive altered states that have deep meaning in the lives of human beings.

Gratefulness

> Give thanks to feelings that have appeared or have been created by you.

When we are grateful we hold onto and enhance uplifting experiences.

Can you remember the last time when you were truly grateful for something? Like when you were given a gift or won something valuable? You felt happiness within and were grateful for the gift received as you smiled that big smile on your face.

Gratefulness allows emotions to become yours to own within you, since you have to acknowledge positive feelings to be grateful for them in the first place.

Take a moment to acknowledge positive memories from your past, the feelings you create now and for the near future. And feel how good it feels to be grateful for them.

Embracement

To accept gratefulness eagerly

To embrace for what you are already grateful for - allows these feelings to grow even stronger inside of you. These can be in the forms showing a feeling of great desire for what is currently being accepted within you or simply raising the bar by embracing what these grateful feelings are made up of.

Embracing positive feelings you are already grateful for allows you to expand them.

Create and acknowledge positive feelings, be grateful and embrace them

Thank you

Thank yourself for your previous embracement

The third part to this is the simple idea of expressing thanks for the whole positive experience. Say thanks and be happy for what you have embraced within yourself and feel satisfied with what you are able to create; this is where acceptance begins to take place.

Have you ever had someone go out of there way to help you with something that really meant a lot to you? Don't you feel satisfied by their actions and automatically feel drawn to say thank you? So why not thank yourself for the GREAT feelings you can make yourself feel in any area of life.

Thank yourself for these empowering accomplishments, decisions and actions that you have embraced in your life to manifest what you really want.

Be grateful, embrace and thank yourself for the feelings you are able to create

Wrap up

Gratefulness - Embracement - Thankfulness

This 'owning positive feelings formula' can be used whenever you become aware of any positive emotion from your unconscious and any feeling you create in your life and imagination.
These emotions stack on top of each other and will make you feel good about yourself anytime you want. Also, use this simple formula to feel even

better about achievements you already have experienced to strengthen and own them within.

Even more; you can do this process with the negative feelings that pop up since you can be grateful for recognizing them when you did, embrace these feelings of gratefulness for helping you to notice what you didn't want, and thank yourself for using this as a **reminder** to focus on what you now **do** want.

Gratefulness - Embracement - Thankfulness

You can now easily make yourself feel good.

Exercise

First take a moment to focus on anything that allows you to feel good

1. Now take a moment to feel grateful for the only fact that you can make yourself feel good right now

2. Embrace this feeling within by realizing the possibility of you being able to make yourself feel even better

3. Thank yourself for the ability to create feelings of making yourself feel good anytime you want to do this exercise

In a nutshell

1. Use this formula to grab onto and strengthen any positive feeling you experience to accept them more easily

2. Be grateful for when negative feelings show up, and embrace yourself for recognizing them when you did, and use them as a reminder of what you want to discover in your life

Positive Pictures and Movies

Every positive thought that you encounter in reaction about subjects on a daily basis is due to the past positive mental rehearsing did before.

Have you ever been to the cinema to watch a new movie and **really** enjoyed it? You may have found yourself driving home talking about it and replaying the exciting scenes in your mind over and over again. You may have watched it a dozen times after that until you knew the best bits off by heart.

When you continue creating positive mental impressions of being successful for the unconscious to recognize as important, they will be processed for you. Most of the time you are not even aware of it and you find yourself suddenly feeling more confident about things.

What kinds of positive movies and images can you create in your mind where you notice yourself behaving happier, more confident, motivated...etc in different areas of life you want?

You can make these images and movies brighter, larger, more colourful, and richer and with more clarity to make them that much more appealing to the unconscious.

You must put beneficial use to enhancing your positive imagination, because it will change your life once you begin to make this a natural part of your everyday awareness.

Exercise

1. Recall a negative scenario in black and white and run it to the end. Pause it, and then rapidly rewind it very quickly and watch everything going backwards very fast to the beginning

2. Now watch yourself in the start of this situation again, but this time doing things in the way you would have liked to do them

3. Make the scene grow bigger in size, brighter, more colourful and with more clarity

6. Step into yourself and feel how good it feels to do things how you should be doing them

Exercise

1. Imagine a round floating ball that would best represent how you feel right now. Notice what colour it is.

- Put this aside for a moment

2. Think of a positive picture or movie with you in it feeling or doing something in the right way you like to

3. Point to where this image is coming from

4. Imagine taking the image and putting it through a laminator, watching it come out shiny and protected.

- Bring your floating ball from earlier back into awareness

5. Notice the laminated picture - next to - your ball of emotions

6. Imagine them being magnetically drawn towards each other, rapping themselves up into one, notice if it has changed shape

6. Take it and put it into your chest as you take in a nice deep breath

Positive Sounds and Voices

We can create and recreate many voices to make us feel empowered.

How would you feel if someone you deeply admire encouraged and praised you in just the right tonality - in moments of the day you really needed it? Imagine hearing this encouraging voice playing in your head over and over again.

Positive voices are very powerful movers and feeling igniters that will change your states easily. Can you remember a time when you heard something funny and just couldn't stop laughing?

Voices from TV shows allow people to experience certain states that move them into action. Your favourite Type of music enables you to dive into particular emotional states and you listen to music for this very reason.

Some of us enjoy listening to relaxing music and nature sounds; hearing the trees swaying in the wind and the distinctive tweeting sound of a bird singing in the distance.

Different sounds and voices makes you feel emotions according to what you have associated to them and can be utilized at WILL.

You have a variety of sounds to choose from that will allow you to experience love, happiness, motivation, relaxation, confidence, passion, desire and just about anything you want.

Pleasant sounds and voices can be linked to certain situations in your life. Search your memory for a positive sound or voice that allows you to feel confident and as you listen to it, think of the situation you desire to feel confident in.

Discover some sounds and voices that make you feel the desired emotions you want. And allow them to radiate through your body and mind.

Exercise

1. Close your eyes and imagine yourself in the situation you want to feel more empowered in

2. Trigger the positive sounds and voices you want and listen to them playing in your head. Mix and match them, hear them go off different times from different places in your mind and feel what they bring. Have fun; listen and feel them radiate through your entire being, in those imagined situations you desire

They can be praising, encouraging, loving, from a TV show or any comment or sound that generates the emotions you deserve. For example: you may want to hear voices of encouragement as you imagine yourself during that important speech. You can hear the wave's crash in on a beach and listen to the sea breeze to relieve stress or anxiety in life. Come up with and use the sounds and voices that are right for you.

Positive Behaviour

Changing the way how you use your body changes the emotional flow you feel within your body because your mind and body are very much linked together.

Have you ever done any acting and got so much into your new positive character that you became this character for a while. It's like you begin to feel different and temporarily forgot who you were. Then as the crowd cheers for you, you get back to reality.

You can literally behave your way into the successful person you desire to be just by doing so; a major talent of which your conscious mind possesses. And can be used despite any feeling or disempowering generalization that gets in the way.

Now let's try a little experiment. Stand up!

Yes I'm talking to you, stand up!

What I want you to do is behave and physically act as if you've just come off the phone after accepting a new job, that you can do standing on your head, which offers £800 a week, just for an hour's work a day!

Purposely walk around with a big smile on your face and use you whole body in a way that represents you are going to feel rich, happy and relaxed for years to come. I want you to physically stand up, use your focus and become engaged in this process for at least 10secs RIGHT NOW!

Can you notice the difference in the way how you feel?

Do you feel different now, compared to how you felt before you started doing this exercise?

Notice you can instantly change the way how you feel just by using your body differently. Imagine if you behaved and physically acted happily like this in relation to your life for a whole week? Would you notice ant difference?

Exercise

1. Come up with a positive phrase that will make you feel stronger. E.g. "I feel happier everyday" "Your confidence is rising"

2. Chant it out load in a rhythm and behave in such a way that represents you are becoming this person as your are saying it

3a. Use rhythm as if you are singing a song. Put your body into overdrive and use your voice and your focus as much as you can to make it real within you RIGHT NOW

3b. Do the same as before, but this time chant as if it has already happened E.g. "I'm already feeling confident" "I knew I was happy" Change your language to be in the future tense and use your body in a way that signifies you already ARE this person. Spend about 5minutes on 3a and 3b.

Exercise two

Talk to yourself and do spontaneous behaviours that you wouldn't normally do to progress in self expression in your life. You can do this alone or in the company of people to gain comfort with any positive feeling you want to feel comfortable with expressing.

You will get to know yourself better. And if you feel uncomfortable; even more reason for why you should do it! When you learn to become comfortable with your silliness and expressing your individuality you will draw closer to your centred self.

What do you want to feel; Motivation, success, love, confidence, happiness? Take your pick and make them a part of your everyday behaviour.

Positive Breathing

Breathing plays an important role in allowing positive emotions to flow within us. Sometimes, muscle groupings within the body, tent to tense up or hold restrictive tension. And these occurrences can be easily freed up with the use of directive breathing.

Alternative breathing will allow you to feel more focus, energized and at peace with yourself. You will be surprised how many people these days don't breathe in a way that represents what they are doing. Through the use of active breathing techniques, an emotional release will flow through you, allowing you to let go of any existing limitations that were once holding you back.

As a whole, breathing affects your emotional state and keeps you in contact with people and the outside world; freeing your conscious and unconscious minds from restrictive thoughts will allow you to feel vibrant in your future endeavours.

Breath of fire

(Read through this once before you do it)

1. Take in a deep breath

2. Exhale and inhale rapidly 10 times through your nose only. As you exhale suck in your abdomen, and as you inhale expand your abdomen out (Count on the exhale)

After the 10th exhale - take in a long deep breathe - and then exhale again out of the mouth (This will prevent you from hyperventilating) then start the cycle again from step 1.

You can do this for as long as you like; if you ever get light headed stop for a moment or two to relax and start again. You can even do this while watching TV. This breathing exercise will help to energize you.

Trains of Thought

Usually we are told to think positive thoughts but have no idea how to start or what to even think about.

The following technique you are about to learn is a great preset positive thinking process you can use to broaden and expand your possibility outlook. The individual steps will enable you to make sense of your life in a new way.

Each of the following steps is executed consecutively to create a train of thought. A train of thought is a string of ideas that easily flow from one to the next, almost like day dreaming a long happy scenario of winning the lottery and spending your winnings. These thoughts are made up of mental movies, sounds and feelings one after the other, without the thought process ever being broken; until somebody comes along and waves their hand in your face.

Let's first go through each step individually to understand the entire process, at the end we'll wrap it all up in a nice little package, ready for future use.

Step one

Beginning thought: Recognizing

To start your new train of thought, recognize subjects that lead to creative ideas that manifest beliefs, reasoning or spring you into action.

Keep coming back to this first step to understand the entire process. It will enable you to gain a sense, of how each of the following steps, string together.

Below are the examples of how you can use positive **dialog** to start a new positive train of thought.

"I am..."

This can be a recognizing of an ability or a made up affirmation that isn't just yet true.

"This feels..."

Being aware of your empowering feelings, and wondering of what else you can potentially make yourself feel.

"You are…"

Telling yourself how happy, wonderful and self assured you are now becoming.

A question

When we ask positive questions we receive positive answers that create trains of thought. E.g. "What is good about feeling good?"

Questions can be used with more precision.

Using these phrases; "I am" "this is" "you are" and a positive question "what is good about this?" <u>can be used about anything in the moment.</u> You can also use these as feel good affirmations. E.g. I feel good! This is wonderful! You are becoming more self assured! How can you become even more self assured? This is the beginning of opening up your mind to what lies ahead.

<u>To start new trains of thought, recognize new positive trains of thought and intentionally create and direct your mind in new positive directions.</u>

You can also use these as feel good affirmations. E.g. I feel good! This is wonderful! You are becoming more self assured! How can you become even more self assured?

Step two

<u>Discovery</u>

After step one, the next step is to open up the original phrase or affirmation.

In other words, take the affirmation "I feel good" and consciously apply it to an area of life you want to imagine yourself feeling good in.

For example "I feel good when washing up" "I feel good when working out" "I feel good when relaxing" Choose an affirmation of your liking and name the situation you would like to apply this affirmation in.

The fact that you are discovering how you can use positive affirmations in those particular situations you want is how they begin to apply in your life.

(Go back to step one and link these two steps together)

Step three

Creativity

Now, during the process of discovery, imagine yourself beginning to create these new feelings and experiences in the situations you have chosen.

For example: If you chose to feel good when working out, Imagine yourself beginning to create feelings of feeling good within you as you are working out in this situation.

(Go back to step one again to mentally link the last three steps together)

Step Five

Effortlessness

Imagine growing in feelings of effortlessness and sensing yourself doing things even more smoothly like you've always wanted to do them, and feeling the creative feelings well up inside of you even more.

What kinds of new effortless thoughts, feelings and behaviours are you easily beginning to get used to in these situations? How much more healthier have you become for your body to look this good?

Effortlessness represents you gradually adapting in those situations you want.

(Create the train of thought all over again from step one)

Step six

Master

Imagine yourself still growing and slowly becoming a master at this. Imagine yourself being efficient - praising and thanking yourself for the powerful feelings that are finally yours. Look in the mirror at your new body with feelings of accomplishment. Realize bright eyed in amazement for how easy it is for you to learn to do anything. Imagine yourself on top of things as if you've been doing this for years now. How much more confident do you think you can become in different situations for the future?

(With these new accomplishments and feelings; how can you use this to loop a new positive train of thought all over again from step one?)
Instead of tripping into a life experience that suddenly triggers these trains of thought because something apparently good has "finally" happened in life,

enabling you to finally think positive about things; why not purposely create these trains of thought RIGHT NOW! Doing this will not only create a mental blue print of success every time that allows you to feel good; but will also train yourself to think **right** regularly in the situations you want. Use this process to become happier in social situation, learn new skills easily to build a sense of freedom in your life.

Wrap up

Realize that each step, from one to six, happens in your mind with the use of your imagination, to create a train of thought. In other words, the steps join up to become" A positive thought process". What most people do is rehearse doing things wrong over and over again in their heads but with this new layout, you can rehearse doing things RIGHT!

Try to experiment and find the most efficient ways that are right for you to gain a sense of the whole process in your very own way. If you feel shy in particular situations, why not try the affirmation "I feel confident" and gradually build on it more good feelings. These are amazing discoveries and will comprehend in your mind leaving positive mental imprints for future success, and will also fill your brain with useful information, just by raising on a positive thought of your choice.

Beware of blocks

Beware of the negative blocks that get in the way of creating positive trains of thought. Do not think any thoughts of doubt or scepticism.

For example: *If I started to think about writing a book but then thought to myself "I'm living in a dream world, this isn't going to work, it's stupid" My positive train of thought becomes broken.*

Never let scepticism get in the way or prevent your success thought processes. Use opened possibility and trains of thought in a way that represents you have an infinite end to them, signifying the dreams you will create for the near future.

Summary

These steps can be done very quickly to gain a sense of the process or you can take some time on each step to really open yourself up.
Take some time to practice with this. You can talk yourself through each step if it makes it any easier. It may also help if you close your eyes, although this is not entirely necessary.

Begin thought (then) Discovery (then) Creativity (then) Effortlessness (then) Master

Begin thought

1. Come up with a phrase or question. E.g. "I can build a business" or "Why am I confident?"

Discover

2. Discover and apply this to what you want. E.g. "What kind of business do I want to run...?" or "What do I want to feel confident in...?

Creativity

3. Imagine yourself creating these feelings in this situation. E.g. "How much more money do I imagine myself making....?" Or "How am I creating even more feelings of confidence in my life...?"

Effortlessness

5. Imagine things are beginning to get more effortless and sense things becoming easier. E.g. "I'm slowly becoming a successful business person and this is beginning to feel easy..." Or "I can't believe how easy I'm beginning to feel more confident in this situation...."

Master

6. Realize you have finally become on top of things. E.g. "I am finally a success and the boss of my life....!" Or "I have literally made myself feel confident in a matter of seconds, I FEEL GREAT...! - Wow, I really can overcome the obstacles in my life (and look back to what you have created)

Remember: Strengthening plans within your head is fine, and will automatically compel you to go out and get it. But why sit around thinking all day when you can decide to use your will right now! **Do both, with some sort of thought and action daily!**

Thank yourself as if you have already thanked yourself - for feeling good.

In a nutshell

1. Learn this process to enhance your creative thinking and you will experience wonderful discoveries in anything you wish to think about

2. Dreams become real with opened possibility in your mind first; new trains of thought will enable you to succeed in anything you put your mind to
3. Learn to use this formula to unlock your inner potential

Your Positive World Is Waiting

Everything starts with emotion, and inside of you there are emotions waiting to explode in you creating what you deserve.

The rat story

There where two rats scurrying around the kitchen looking for food because no 'humans' were around. They managed to run into a small cup of cream which was considered to be a tasty treat. They began sipping the cream from the rim of the cup, managing to get tiny sips without knocking it over.

The rat named Bert was a bit greedy and so climbed up to the rim of the cup to get some more. Accidentally he falls in and begins to drown - really trying hard to get out. Clyde (the other rat) screams "It's useless, just give up mate, your wishing for the impossible!" Soon enough though Bert continuous to scurry and kick his little legs until the cream slowly becomes thick enough enabling Bert to finally free himself from drowning.

If you don't give up on what you want, you will eventually get it!

If you were in Bert's shoes what would you do?

Would you give up and die? Or kick your little legs and never give up?

The things we need to focus on and take some sort of daily action towards growing our higher self esteem are as follows:

1. Your worth and what you deserve

This is everything that you dream about; just like everybody else and getting to that stage where enough is enough. And reaching that point of doing whatever it takes to succeed.

2. Possibility

The huge amounts of possibility we have and the choices we can make that allow us to grow and completely change our lives. This must be exercised to broaden our range in life, just like how many people have already learned to do so.

3. Your capability

What you believe you are capable of (which is anything you put your mind to). Another key learning that must be adapted for you to grow and become stronger willed inside.

4. Ideas

There are many positive directions in which your train of thought can go, to help you come up with new discoveries that serve you. By contemplating on moments of the day with yourself anytime you can, will slowly have dramatic effects in your life. You will eventually gain a broader foundation of success thinking.

5. Practice

As they say, practice makes perfect! And it does since you can only improve when you practice; whether if you practice in new thoughts, behaviours or feelings. You will gain enormous when you take individual time to practice in all of them - taking on the attitude of **always learning** something new whether your actions work or not.

Discover what you want

Here are some useful questions you can ask yourself to lead you in the right directions. Grab a pencil or actively participate if necessary.

Name two emotional reactions to external influence that you want to get rid of.

1.

2.

Why do you want to get rid of them? List some reasons.

1.

2.

What do you want to achieve in life?

1.

2.

Why do you want to achieve this?

1.

2.

Why should you do everything within your control to make this your new positive reality? And how is it going to feel when you have?

1.

2.

How is it going to feel when you have it?

1.

2.

Think - in agreement, of creating the feelings and behaviours which will encourage you, to pursue what you want.

Behave - in agreement with the thoughts and feelings that will allow you to achieve what you desire.

Feel - in agreement of what thoughts and behaviours allow you to feel.

The you inside – is grateful for you

You are grateful for the you inside

This gratefulness - is shared between you

Exercise

1. Close your eyes and take a deep breath in and out

2. Imagine a 10 foot juicer in front of you

3. Choose four types of fruit and attach some positive emotions to them, E.g. Watermelon = Feelings of financial abundance: Strawberry = Relaxation: Banana = Confidence: Apple = Motivation for achieving your goals

4. After you have all your fruits linked to the emotions you want, throw the fruitful emotions into the juicer and mix them up. Watch the colour of the liquid change as all the positive emotions mix together

5. Raise the juicer above your head and pour this juice through the top of your head - filling yourself up to the brim. Feel the juicy sensations all throughout your body

Rehearse and Manifest

The way how you feel in the morning about yourself determines the rate of which you set the rest of your day up for success.

This is the first POWER MOVE you MUST do, to immediately take action as soon as you wake up!

This demonstrates your ability to take full control of your life - to break through hesitation and grab hold of your individual power to create a new life!

The four main important areas in which we need to rehearse and set ourselves up for success each day are as follows:

Mental

To condition your mind for success in terms of focus and using your imagination effectively by placing your attention upon your desires, feeling unshaken by doubt or scepticism - learning from failure; and realizing anything you consciously use in your life will undoubtedly manifest.

Body

The ability to use your body in the directions that serve you and to become comfortable with using your desired behavioural habits whenever you please.

Love Life

Feeling appreciative for the beneficial and beautiful growing connections with people; the qualities and opportunities that is in the world for you to choose and grow with - throughout every area of your life.

Self

Your inner self is the place within you that is untapped by social conditioning; this place within that you are connecting with to experience a sense of becoming closer with your inner purity as a human being.

To prepare yourself for rehearsing wake up an hour early each day, or schedule 30mins or 15mins with yourself any time you can. The more time you give to yourself, the clearer and more empowered you will become in manifesting your destiny.

If you like you can start with 5 minutes for the first day and then build every 5 minutes each consecutive day, as you gain a stronger sense of recognition on how much THIS benefits your life.

The manifestation process

With this process you can use the techniques you have learned throughout this book and also contribute some of your own ideas.

1. Get straight out of bed in the morning without any hesitation

2. Lay out your dreams and goals in mind or write them down. KNOW what you are setting out to manifest today. What do you want to grow stronger in? What do you want to learn, create and discover in your life? Create your day mentally by building on what you want to strengthen within yourself for the rest of the day. How do you want to feel after this day has ended?

3. Move your body (preferably outside) in a way that allows you to feel at peace with your self. Focus on moving and feeling in the way that connects them both together, moving towards your desires (motivated or passionate towards your goals) this allows you to move in conjunction with what you want. You can also workout while doing this whole process if you have the time

4. Appreciate the beautiful life you truly possess right now as being a part of who you are in this living breathing moment; we ARE life. Being alive is an opportunity, so be grateful for the experience of love that you feel and the connections you share with others. Close your eyes for a moment and think about all the people you love in your life and all the people that love you. Manifest in how wonderful this feels and how wonderful your life is going to feel with more love in it.

Close your eyes for a moment and quite your mind. Discover in who you are today as a person and the unique and special qualities about you. Become in touch with your purity as a human being, whatever you discover that is right for you.

Your own views, opinions, desires and even dreams will always alter and change according to your own individual growth - and this is how you grow; YOU LEARN and DISCOVER in life to be the complete person you seek to become.

5. **Self:** Purity, unmixed, flawless, uncontaminated, squeaky clean, complete, unpolluted, natural, genuine, untainted, wholesome; your authentic self! (Collins dictionary and thesaurus)

You may not know what your destiny and spirit is just yet but discovering and taking time for your self will allow you to find it.

6. After you finish step five be grateful, embrace and give thanks to yourself for this entire experience at least 10times over. Feel energized and thankful for what you are setting out to achieve today.

You can sing along to a victory song and pretend you're the superhero and saviour of your day. SET YOUR DAY UP FOR SUCCESS AND MANIFEST YOUR DREAMS!

Drawing to the end of your days accomplishments; be thankful for the moments you were able to create earlier, no matter how small or AMAZINGLY BRILLIANT they were.

Lie in bed and thank yourself for what you have gained as if you have ALREADY thanked yourself for it, and keep doing this over and over again.

You are the creator of your life and you are the creator of each new day from the second you open your eyes.

Summary

1. Get straight out of bed

2. Lay out the sort of day you want to create, the dreams and goals you are aiming to manifest for this day

3. Move your body (Outside) to become one and at peace with yourself. Move and focus in relation towards going after and achieving your goals

4. Manifest in the love you have for your life - and the love you have for the lives of others

5. Discover in your self purity, destiny and general life to become in touch with your inner purpose and humility

6. Be grateful - embrace and be thankful for this uplifting process, feeling energized and healthy for the day that lies ahead. Celebrate in anyway you can to own your self victories

7. At the end of your successful days as you lay in bed, contemplate on all the achievements you have made so far; in a way that allows you to feel grateful for the opportunity to live a happier life style

PART FIVE

HANDLING PEOPLE AND YOUR EXTERNAL REALITY

Our Views

People do not necessarily set out to ruin our lives, and even though some do - it doesn't mean we should put up with it just because they have different views compared to our own.

Everyone looks at the external world in their own different and unique way.

IF we view people and the opportunities in life in a way that makes us feel we **can succeed** this is what we'll experience. It's a given!

The outside world is basically what you think it is. In other words, whatever you create in your own head and associate to people, self esteem, money, tasks, life goals...etc. You will believe it to be true and will act accordingly, because your mind doesn't know the difference between what you perceive as being real, and what you don't perceive as real. It picks up on everything you perceive nevertheless! In other words, if you perceive something as not being real that's what you'll experience.

However you choose use to perceive your external reality it will trigger your mind to look out for things it relates to. If you view a vulnerable situation as a means to create security, your mind will automatically come up with new ideas in conjunction with your external world to create the views you want.

Since the mind reacts to external influences in this way; you can use this to purposely perceive external situations in a positive way, so you bring up new ideas and tools as to what you are consciously looking for.

You can use this as proof that you can learn to view things differently. Through practicing the techniques your about to learn, they will serve you automatically when you need them.

Realize if somebody out there is trying to put you down or trying to stop you from growing, they are just using their learned beliefs, views, behaviours, opinions etc, according to what they have learnt during their own lives. So what's the point in arguing with something that you cannot ever control?

Take the idea upon yourself, for your own reasons that there are no **right** or **wrong** opinions or habits.

There are only habits that serve us or don't serve us as individuals, and other people's habits usually run out of habit anyway! This gives you the upper hand because most people are not aware of their views.

Changing your views, changes your frame of mind.

Set out to gain personal control, by switching the inner controls of what you perceive your external reality to be.

You are an equal human being on this planet just like everybody else. You should be lucky you're not a fish or you'll probably be in serious trouble.

Exercise

This exercise is used to respond differently towards those particular 'things' people do that may bug you or put a dampen on your positive emotional states and/or overall success.

1. Close your eyes and relax by taking in a deep breath

2. Think of the person that puts a dampen on your emotions in a specific situation you want

3. Now begin to perceive them in a way that is beneficial to you. Recognize all the new positive thoughts and feelings that they have about you. How would they view you in a way that makes you feel good about them and yourself?

4. Now, dissociate from yourself and step into this person for a second, and experience the new feelings that they have for you as you look through their eyes at yourself

5. Once you feel comfortable. Step out of them - back into yourself, and feel the positive difference in how you view that person and how they feel towards you

Counter technique

You can use this technique whenever someone is verbally attacking you

1. While someone is verbally attacking you IGNORE THEM. And focus on the way how you want to feel instead (Preferably the opposite of how their attacks make you feel)

In other words, block off their attacks and redirect your focus towards how you want to feel despite what they say

Use focus in different directions when verbal attacks are made. Never blindly accept an attack or let it affect you. Practice!

When someone says something to you which you undoubtedly know isn't true. You usually focus on **your** truth, instead of what they may think. So always focus on what you want to be true for you, and never consider outside negative jargon people offer you.

Something is only true when it is true for you. So create your own empowering truths and stick with them in a way that protects your growing self esteem

Behaviour exercise

Behave in a way that makes you feel empowered, in reaction to other people's negative behaviour.

You can do this with a tapping of the finger, swaying of your body, tapping your heel or even clenching your buttocks. Do this in a way that is not offensive, mocking or patronising others. Rather do it in a way that represents you are using your body despite the negative emotions they are projecting, to gain a sense of inner control and centeredness within.

Play with your behaviour; move, focus and feel in a way that allows you to feel the emotions you desire, when and **if** negative situations arise.

In a nutshell

1. People are human just like you and have nothing over you! You can learn anything and everything that they have and also what they don't even know how to get

2. All of us have habits that we don't even necessarily want - and most of us generally act out of habit anyway

3. Respect others for what they have learnt, and continue to set out in becoming the self assured higher self esteemed person **you** are aiming to be

4. Your self value always comes first and this self value will allow you to notice the values in others

They Wish They Were As Amazing As You

A great way into protecting yourself from negative external influences that sometimes come your way is to review them in a positive way that makes their actions seem like a cry for help - as they wish they were as amazing as you.

You can think, feel and do things for yourself. You have learnt to understand how your mind works, and journey towards something amazing for your life. You contribute to your life and others life's in your very own unique way.

YOU ARE AMAZING!

Do you really think someone else is more amazing than your own soul?

You may not feel what others feel, nor have what others have at this moment - and there is no need to be jealous either; Because you can feel what **you** feel and gain what **you** want, according to your own desires, in your very own unique way that nobody else can create like **you** can.

Recognize what makes you amazing in your own special way. Whenever someone is negative towards you; fall back on the fact that they are crying for help - as they wish they had the astounding positive unique qualities that you now have. You are a unique individual and this is what separates your own inner being and characteristics that make you up as a person.

When you really begin to discover, you are a unique human being that possesses certain individual qualities that I don't or anybody else can experience the way how **you** individually experience them; you can use this to justify who you really are - and **who** you are really becoming. And if people ever attack you this only validates their cries for help.

Heck I wish I was as amazing as you because you have certain personality traits and qualities that I don't have in my life.

"Can I have them please?"

Seriously: Embrace your personal amazing qualities and positive feelings in any way you can, that allows you to feel protected from external influences that you didn't want.

You are an individual, and **you** truly **are** amazing!

Exercise

A great way into gaining that feeling of they wishing they were as amazing as you is to practice.

1. Make a list of some qualities, thoughts, habits, behaviours and goals that make you amazingly unique. Feel these amazing qualities you have radiate inside of you

2. Think of the person that attacks you and imagine their attacks coming out squeaky or silly. Notice how it doesn't affect you and all you feel is your positive experience of embracing your own individual qualities and characteristics

Feel people's negative attacks as they wish there were as amazing as you.

In a nutshell

1. You are your own person and you are individually unique. And no one can do anything the way you do them

2. Your wonderful personality, qualities, characteristics and positive mental processes are yours and this makes you amazing in your own right. Nobody can take this away from you except one person, YOU!

How to Develop Rapport

What is rapport?

Rapport is the feeling of being comfortable with someone, experiencing a bond or an understanding in views.

It is showing others by your behaviour and words that you accept the validity of their experience for them.

There are friends and family that you feel comfortable with, these people you have rapport with. But you don't have rapport with a stranger on the street.

Rapport is built on an unconscious understanding of **connection** and **comfort**. When people are in rapport together there is a flow, like a dance exchanging similar patterns of body language, expressions, voice tempo and/or volume.

Rapport creates a basis for co-operative communication.

If you can imagine a group of people in a room talking together, could you notice which people are in rapport and which are not?

You can easily notice who is in rapport by the level of comfort and natural flowing conversations they are having. **When people are like each other, they like each other** as they share on some level an understanding in views.

Imagine if two strangers began dancing together for the first time in a rhythmic motion, it is without a doubt that rapport will gradually gain as they adapt to one another's energy and behaviour in music.

If one of them danced out of tune no rapport will be gained because there will be a mismatch in body language, tempo, emotions...etc. **This indicates a misunderstanding in views.**

To gain rapport then, we must stay in tuned with their pace of conversation by echoing their postures, vitality and charisma. In a sense you can gain rapport with others very effectively by joining their own personal dance.

Learning how to build rapport will enable you to gain mutual comfort with virtually anyone very rapidly.

To establish rapport naturally and respectfully pace their ongoing reality; In other words, if they are fast, move fast and if they are slow, go slow and always reflect their pace. You will project a powerful message of interest for them, which allows them to feel valued by you. This is how we naturally gain

rapport anyway, but for the most part everything happens outside of our conscious awareness.
What would it be like if you could gain stronger rapport with your boss, loved one or maybe a new friend you would like to meet?

Rapport building is very useful when trying to sell, encourage, negotiate, flirt and for socialize.

The dance will be harmonious, built between your integrity and purpose to build a bridge to another person's experience of the world.

Matching gesture

Matching gestures and body language is a great way to build rapport. We all naturally enjoy being in the company of others that are in tune with our own body language.

Slight gestures can be matched in opposite of limbs. If someone makes a small hand gesture you can twitch your nose. A nod of the head can be matched with a small shoulder shrug.

To be effective at this you must be aware of how people are using their bodies. Practice with someone and use your peripheral vision to open up your awareness. Matching does not need to be done exactly on time; rather you can be up to 20 to 45 seconds behind. You don't have to match in the exact same way either; you can match one quarter of their initial movement and still be effective.

When we are interacting we are usually not aware of these minute matches in movement and when this is happening all the time, on an unconscious level, a connection begins to emerge. You just get that feeling of "hey this person understands me!"

Note: Fidgety movements are not to be matched and/or other extreme behaviours. You want to pace that persons ongoing reality, not mock them.

Notice

A twitch of the nose can be matched with a twitch of the shoulders.

A sneeze can be matched with a slight gasp of breath.

A matching in the rhythm of walking in steps is a great rapport builder. (Not exactly the same, but in rhythm)

A tapping of the foot can be matched with a tatting of the tongue.

Be sure to copy slightly, not exactly, and match 10-45 seconds after you have picked up on something; practice to make this an unconscious habit. Be subtle and have fun - as you naturally connect with others.

Voice

Voice speed, rhythm and volume can also be matched to build rapport.

If a very loud person were talking to a very quite person there would be a slight mismatch in views. But when you delicately match someone's volume of speech_ rapport can be gained in this way.

You can try varying the rhythm and tempo of your speech. Fast talking people enjoy talking to someone that can match their pace, rather than speaking with someone that communicates at a slower pace.

People speak at the rate they understand! So speak at their rate to be understood.

Notice

Volume - Speak loudly or quietly

Rhythm and tempo - Fast or slow, fluent or pausing

Note: Do not match stammering or speech impediments

Positive questions

Questions that lead to positive directions in thought allow other people to express themselves - and this is also a great way to gain rapport.

We enjoy talking about ourselves and when we are asked questions that revolve around our uplifting subjects and qualities, we begin to open up and express our personalities more; to which we usually associate these positive feelings with the person that is asking.

To gain a lead into asking questions you must notice what the person likes talking about, then ask questions that revolve around the subject to heighten their possibility and self expression. These subjects can revolve around future dreams, pleasant experiences, what they really enjoy, past accomplishments...etc

If someone had an amazing day and you asked "what was amazing about it?" they will begin to relive the experience and feelings all over again.

You will easily be able to notice the positive effects your questions are having.

Just make sure you don't ask questions that lead to negative experiences. E.g. "Why are you so useless?"

Positive questions

What did you like about that?

How much more fun do you think you can have?

Wow that's great, what was it like then...?

You enjoyed that didn't you?

These questions initiate positive thoughts and self expressions which create pleasant environments and conversations that expand rapport.

Have fun

Matching may feel weird at first, but you will soon realize building rapport is fun. Go out there and try it, you'll be surprised at the results. When you gain comfortable feelings in doing this, people will open up to you and share their world as stronger connections begin to build.

You can also encourage people that are feeling low by building rapport - and then slowly leading them in new directions to make them feel better.

When someone is down you can ask "What can we do right now for you to feel better?" or "Hey, do you remember that time when we...?"

Once you change your own energy and rhythm, others will naturally tag along since a connection has **already** been established.

It's something enjoyable that we can do, to develop a growing sense of connection with people through our dignity and respect for others.

Don't take my word for it! Go out there and notice what happens when you match others and notice what happens when you stop. Learn to be subtle in your approach and make using these techniques a natural part of your daily awareness. Pace even longer than you think you need to and observe closely for the signs of that person feeling at ease with you.

You may ask: What if I'm in a group of people?

Match and gain rapport with the person that has the highest energy and influence on the overall group.

In a nutshell

1. You can gain rapport by respectfully pacing and matching behaviour, voice tempo and volume. You can also ask positive questions that allow people to express themselves in self fulfilling ways

2. Rapport is gained by making people feel valued by you, with the use of rapport building

3. Gaining rapport is a fun process we naturally do when we get to know each other. So why not do it on purpose to create comfortable environments? Move at their pace and have fun with interacting with others!

Communication

How do we become effective communicators?

Communication is a word that describes many things.

We teach, negotiate and have casual conversations during communication. These different types of communication have their own individual effects and outcomes and are perceived in many different ways.

When we communicate we perceive what the other person is saying and then react according to our own thoughts and feelings.

Have you ever had someone really upset you, and they responded with "I didn't mean it in that way!" this can be a result of you perceiving the communication in a way that wasn't intended, or the person communicating to you in a way that couldn't get the right message across.

All of us express different shades of meaning in everyday conversation. However, it's not **what** we say that makes the difference, but how we say it that determines our results.

Communication does not only involve words as many people are led to believe. Rather our words have the least impact when we use communication. Our behaviour and tonality play the the BIGGER roles!

<u>This is a diagram based on what makes up the effectiveness of overall communication.</u>

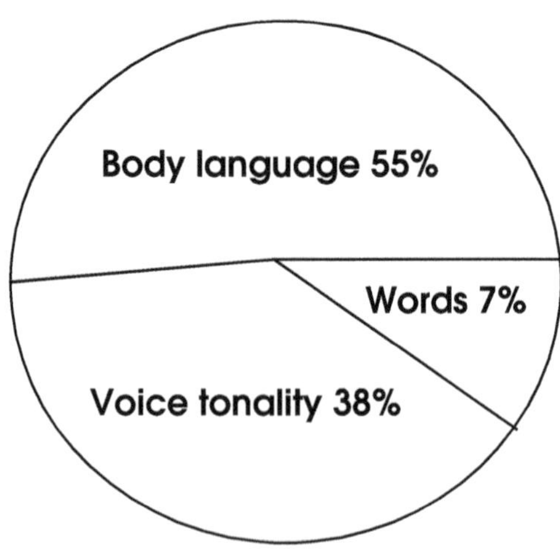

Sometimes even using tonality, body language and words effectively may end up in a different response compared to what we hoped for. This is why varying our behaviours and tonality will gain a bigger chance of landing our messages across more clearly.

Tonality

To speak to one another in general conversation we must use tonality; otherwise we wouldn't know the feelings being expressed behind the words we use.

Consider this in the form of question and statement. "Ben walked across the room" is a statement.

"Ben walked across the room?" which is a question, uses tonality to put the original message across in a different way. Otherwise it wouldn't be perceived as a question at all.

This principle is the same when you use tonality in other contexts.

Imagine if you were having an argument with someone very aggressively, then purposely changed the tonality of what you were saying to a 'peace making' tonality. Do you think the person receiving this type of communication will feel different towards you?

The recipient is most likely to perceive your tonality as a means to what you are suggesting.

Let's now experiment this with a small sentence "It's a rainy day"

Say these words with a happy tonality "It's a rainy day"

Now say the same phrase in a sad tonality "It's a rainy day"

Now say the phrase in a passionate tonality "It's a rainy day"

If you use different tonalities with what you are saying the person receiving this communication is likely to react to the varying use of your tonality.

The emotional impact you would like to convey will allow others to pick up on the underlying meaning of what your words mean.

Practice playing with the use of your tonality as part of your everyday communication, you will slowly gain a freedom in self expression and will become better at putting your messages across more easily.

Body language

Behaviour plays the biggest role during communication - and is considered most influential. Just like tonality, the recipient will perceive your body language as a means to what you are suggesting.

If you said to someone "I made a million pounds" but had the body posture of someone that looks depressed. The person being spoken to would probably react with "What's the matter with you, you just won a million pounds!?"

But if you jumped around in excitement the person will instantly know what you are trying to say.

Let's try a little experiment:

Take a moment to say the words "You are great!" and use your body in a way that represents you are agreeing with someone.

Now say "you are great" again, but this time stick your middle fingers up to use cursing gestures.

Now say the phrase "you are great" and use your body to convey the messages of feeling sexy and flirting.

It is without a doubt that body language plays an important role in not only how you perceive others communication, but also, how your overall communication is perceived by others.

There are no specific behaviours or gestures that are mandatory when using your body language to put your desired messages across.

Confidence, comfort, connection, appreciation, warmth, agreement and love...; Use your body language to convey the messages you want in anyway that feels natural to you and practice projecting them out. People will generally warm up to what you are trying to say with your body and will process what you are doing subliminally.

Wrap up

When communicating with someone, we must not get discouraged if our communication was perceived in a way we didn't hope. There is no guarantee that the person will always receive your messages clearly.

Instead you must have an overall outcome for what you are trying to communicate, notice what responses you are getting and continue to change what you do or say until you get a desired result or resolution.

Communication is a great tool and can be explored in many effective ways.

Do you know someone in your life that radiates a very friendly warm energy? By using communication effectively, you can radiate any energy you choose.

In a nutshell

1. Accompanied with words, your body language and tonality highly determine the effectiveness of your overall communication

2. Practice using congruent tonality and body language to convey the desired messages you want: whether if you are teaching, flirting, negotiating, socializing...etc.

3. The meaning of your overall communication is the results you are getting, if your communication is perceived in the wrong way or you're not getting the results you want, try something else. This is also very useful in business and selling.

Flowing Conversation

Can you remember the last time when you where enjoying the company of someone so much that everything around your environment just seemed to disappear? You weren't aware of it anymore, just fixed on the enjoyment occurring right in front of you.

This experience is a flowing conversation.

Some people have trouble with reaching this stage of flow because they are either too focused on themselves or concerned with what the other person is thinking. There are also times when become at ease and everything becomes a natural flow of communication, almost as if we warm up to people easily.

Flow is like water trickling down a stream - the ride becomes smoother and easier as you go down and these states of flow are naturally within us all.

The key here is to strengthen this natural flowing state within you, to the point where these states automatically ignite when you're not aware of it - and this will set you free from conversational blocks.

To gain flow we must focus on beneficial outcomes for our overall interactions.

For this to work effectively you must create a goal that allows both of you during rapport building to feel good together. For example: "Let's have fun!" is a positive goal. "We can share our positive energies" is a positive goal. This will enable flowing communication to run smoothly.

When two people are in flow they are usually contributing the same things.

To gain flowing conversation then, you must assign (in your imagination) a shared positive goal with that person. This means, the person already wants to connect with you in the way you want, all you need to do is practice connecting to your shared goal with the use of your body language and tonality.

You can use this technique to become more confident, flirtatious and just about anything you want according to the positive shared goals you choose.

<u>Imagine this is a person you are communicating with.</u>

The feelings you want to experience is felt between you because you are both contributing the same thing. (According to you that is) Hence, the other person will naturally join in with you.

Do you know someone who manages to effortlessly establish flowing conversations? This is mainly because this person has learned to use their mind and body as one during overall communication. They have learned to naturally focus on their general outcomes while not being aware of what they are doing anymore. And this is what you are learning to do, to feel good as you communicate and this allows you others to feel good as well.

Assign different goals to the different people and different categories of people you want to flow with. Always adapt towards your goals and learn from mistakes, until you become effective at creating flowing feelings with ease.

With practice, you will soon learn to view overall interactions in new flowing ways.

Practice alone

This exercise is to be practiced alone to gain an inner flow with yourself, with the use of your imagination.

1. Imagine the person or people you want to flow with. (Whether if it's being effective in influencing, teaching, socializing etc) And think of what category of people they fall under (Rich, sad, good looking, strand-offish etc)

2. Create an outcome or overall goal that you want to create and project towards the overall situation in a way that benefits you both

3. Now imagine speaking with them using your body language, tonality and focus to enhance the feelings of the overall situation. You may notice the person you imagine yourself communicating with responding to you in positive reaction to the positive goal you are manifesting with them.

4. Gain comfort with using your mind and body together and congruently with the feelings your goal creates in a harmonious way

You can also practice with your life goals too, to feel even more like the successful person you are becoming.

Just do the exercise again, but this time, replace the person with a positive goal you want to achieve in. Imagine building your mind and body connection with the feelings your goal creates until you find yourself thinking, feeling and behaving in terms of effortlessly creating flow.

Practice with people

Practicing with other people is a great way for you to learn faster.

You can invite a friend to play "the flowing game" where you both experiment with different positive states of flow.

You can mix and match positive goals to see the effects
Example: "I feel great" and your friend "I feel motivated to succeed"

1. Both of you come up with a positive goal you want to strengthen and project towards each other to experience a state of flow

E.g. "I feel great" and for your friend "I feel motivated to succeed"

2. Now use flowing conversation with one another, using your communication and focus to strengthen the flowing states you have set for yourselves

You can even test each other by throwing out some challenging comments while you interact. This will enable you to learn how to deal with real life situations to keep your emotional outcomes intact. Speak to each other naturally and realize from now on you both have a positive goal attached to one another until you both agree to stop it. Do this for weeks together if you like and watch what happens.

Wrap up

Once you have learned to socialize with different emotions, and have begun to strengthen your mind and body connection with yourself, towards how you want to flow in life. You will grow to find everything becoming less of an effort to achieve and your flow will happen automatically.

If you feel uncomfortable practicing at certain stages. Get used to practicing this by first using focus alone, with maybe a little bit of body language and tonality by mixing and matching, until you find your desired states. Start from whatever you feel comfortable with and then **build** to fill those gaps within.

Be sure not to violate someone's emotional limit, it is disrespectful to take advantage of others feelings just to fulfil your own.

In a nutshell

1. Flowing conversation is a result of strong connections being made between people

2. While communicating, your positive goals emotions are contributed between you with the use of your body language and tonality

3. Practice generating positive shared outcomes during your communication to move towards them and to make others feel good around you

Receive the Gift of Connection

When someone tries to understand you, doesn't test your limits and makes you feel good during low times - when they are affirmative, understanding and strong willed how does it feel?

Does it feel good to have someone with higher self esteem looking out for your well being to comfort you whenever emotionally disturbed? **Can you imagine if this person were now you?**

Since all humans need to experience this connection you can feel good since most people around you crave for connection **from you** too.

Every one of us as human beings want to be encouraged, supported, taught, motivated and experience new loving connections with one another. Having friends that contribute to our lives in a positive way makes us happy. We crave for more people to understand our world; after all we love being understood don't we?

There is actually a space inside all human beings that longs to experience an overwhelming connection with everyone. This space inside becomes more fulfilled as more people want to connect with you. This brings about new adventures, experiences, ideas and growing friendships that lay ahead.

When you feel that others are longing for your connection, you will have no reason to feel withdrawn anymore - as we all alike want to experience uplifting connections too.

Feel excited since what they want, and everybody else truly wants, is what you want also, TO FEEL CONNECTED!

This can even be used as a flowing goal or outcome. "We all crave for connection"

To strengthen the feelings of receiving the gift of connection, we must practice the notion of already feeling connected to one another in an uplifting way.

Exercise

1. Close your eyes and think of someone you want to connect with: Imagine this person radiating "a need for connection" towards you.

Really notice how it feels to be needed by someone

3. Imagine a beam of light travelling from their solar plexus to yours.

You may feel a click to realize a connection has been made

4. Feel a sense of appreciation for making the connection and say: "thank you for needing my connection"

Exercise

Play a game with a friend and exchange positive complements to each other; Great fun, especially in a group. This will also heighten the moral of the room not to mention everyone's higher self esteem.

These compliments can be about anything you like. Whoever runs out of compliments to give back loses.

In a nutshell

1. We all deserve to experience fulfilling, uplifting, trustful connections with one another. Since we all deeply desire this, connect and reach out to this need within others

2. People crave for your connection and love, and you do to. So spread love in your life to the people around you wherever you may go

3. Believe in yourself and also help others to believe in themselves too; share your growth in higher self esteem

Touch

When we are touched in different ways we feel different emotions. A delicate stroke of the face generates different feelings compared to being pinched by someone. Physical human contact naturally makes us feel more comfortable together, consciously or unconsciously.

When you have physical human contact you **will** gain rapport!

Physical contact can also be referred to as "Kino" - this represents kinaesthetic (or feeling) descriptions.

Anchoring

An anchor is an emotional reaction to stimuli.

When we are in a certain emotional state, we sometimes link up these states to a physical touch, picture or sound. So if whenever we see, hear or get touched in that same way again, we automatically go back into that emotional state from before.

Can you recall a photograph taken of you as a child that allows you to go back into a particular emotional state?

Have you ever really fancied someone and had a special song that reminded you of them? This song is an anchor because whenever you hear that song again, you immediately go back into that emotional state.

The more this is reinforced the stronger the anchor becomes.

This means whenever you physically touch someone while they are in a positive emotional state, they will associate these positive emotions towards your touch, and so an anchor will be created.

This means you can make others feel significantly better by your physical touch and general overall presence.

Putting our hands on a persons shoulder, giving a hug, a handshake, a tap on the arm and overall playful body language are all suitable examples.

To use this effectively, link different touches to different emotions. If someone is feeling happy you can touch them on the shoulder, if someone is feeling excited you can tap them on the arm and so on...use anchoring to grab onto positive emotional states. People will feel good about you being around to enhance their personal enjoyment.

After you have established some anchors, you can use this to comfort others if they ever feel low. Just repeat your positive touch from earlier, and this will fire of the good feelings all over again in a subtle way that allows them to feel good.

Anchor positive emotional states, and trigger them off when you would like someone to feel them again.

Another tip to make others feel good around you is to practice smiling. Smiling makes you happy and we all have better days when we are smiled at for no apparent reason. You can smile at strangers, this starts new conversations and can better someone's day. You can even flirt and start new relationships with a smile.

Seek enjoyment out of an everyday smile.

People react with "Who me?" or "Hi yourself..." Spread happiness by spreading the gift of touch, and smile in your overall happiness for being alive. Be happy in life and cherish the moments you have with the people around you in anyway you can.

Exercise

(Read through this once before you do it)

1. Think of some emotions you would like to instantly trigger within you when you want them. Confidence, relaxation, sexy etc

2. Imagine yourself feeling these emotions in the situations you want. Make the images and movies big, bright and bold and hear the positive sounds and voices echoing through you. And when these feelings become strong enough, squeeze your wrist. Repeat 3 times to create a powerful anchor on yourself

3. Whenever you need to feel this good again, just repeat the same touch to trigger the some positive feelings. The anchor always generates the emotions it's linked to.

Live exercise

In a real life situation the most appropriate places to touch people you are meeting for the first time are as follows:

First: A tap on the wrist (Move in close)

Second: A hand on the arm

Third: A rub on the back or shoulder

Fourth: Holding hands in some way

1. Use these steps one after the other to anchor some positive feelings e.g. Happiness, comfort, excitement, fascination etc. if you already know the person, anchor from wherever you want. You can fire off previously set anchors whenever you think is most appropriate.

Flow with your overall communication along with everything else you have learned up until now.

In a nutshell

1. Kino gains rapport and casual comfort

2. An anchor is a reaction of emotion linked to a touch, picture or sound

3. Purposely create positive anchors on yourself to bring back those empowering states when you need them

4. Use anchors with other people and fire them off again and again to make them feel good

5. Smile at life and at others, spread happiness and happiness will return to you

PART SIX

THE TIME HAS COME

The Real Challenge in Life

These days most people lead themselves to believe they should conquer others to succeed in life. **Supposedly** this is the biggest challenge in life but this is simply not true, since it does not allow us to gain a sense of self justification.

What is the real beneficial challenge you have to become so much stronger within that contributes to your growing self esteem?

Martial artists are taught **not** to use their hard earned ability to conquer others. Rather they are taught to conquer themselves to gain true discipline, respect and self control. If they monitored their ability based on others expectations they wouldn't be able to unleash their real inner strength, overcome struggles and break bricks with their heads!

It's only the struggling journey of conquering ourselves that we soon enough see results from the inside out and during any type of training this is a key principle to have.

The more you challenge yourself and really have fun in the journey of growing to become more; your efforts become an inner graceful power which you can decide to keep a secret. It's the same notion of being free of self doubt and **already** knowing what you can **really** do, despite what other people may think or say.

Everything becomes internal, along with the GRACEFUL EXPECTATIONS you have placed upon yourself.

Continue to test your will to succeed and you **will** undoubtedly gain what you want. The harder you push, the faster you will become. And during this process of special uplifting moments of achievement; keep these moments to yourself and realize you are creating something new within your self for the future.

An amateur gardener on his first day was very excited to learn about gardening. His first lesson was learning to plant rice, and this was the first stepping stone of achieving his apprenticeship. With confidence, the fresh bulbs of rice were laid out by hand and planted with lightning light speed.

However, little did he know that the rice had to be planted in intercepting vertical and horizontal lines like a chess board, having a 15cm gap between each squared point. He was told to redo them. His teacher then smiled at him and said "rice needs space to grow, just like humans, that's why we must respect each other".

When rice grows it drops seeds and grows even more rice around the area. Planting rice too close together causes messy uneven crops. And this is what can happen if we make conquering others our main life's concern.

To be successful in life then, is to space yourself out with respect! So you can have your own little world of internal growth, to drop positive seeds that affect your surroundings in an uplifting way.

When you respect people for who **they** are, it allows you to spend time with growing and discovering who **you are** becoming.

Imagine if you never became angry and never became upset in relation to what other people thought or did, and respected their view of the world by not resenting, hating or being jealous of them.

You will gain the upper hand in life based on you becoming non-effected by disempowering external influences that 'try' ruin your own positive internal experience. This gives you the time and space to create powerful hidden feelings that keep you zealous in your endeavours.

It is important for your overall respect to keep certain positive experiences to yourself - to independently build on them within you to expand your self esteem.

This is where the true power of success in every area of your life lies, WITHIN: Conquer your inner world according to what you want because this is the biggest and most rewarding challenge in life - eventually representing that you **can** succeed!

Do whatever it takes to conquer your inner world and feel that true inner sense of power exploding from within, whether it being emotionally, spiritually, financially and/or health wise.

GO AFTER YOUR DREAMS RIGHT NOW! NO MATTER WHAT IT TAKES!
EMPOWER YOUR DESTINY TOWARDS REACHING SUCCESS!

In a nutshell

1. Trying to conquer others won't make you become stronger; it will only create an arrogant illusion contradicting **pure** internal truth. Instead conquer **your own** goals, dreams, body and emotions.

2. Overcome your very own limits, due to your own efforts. Make a pact to never give up on yourself and set out to achieve what you rightfully deserve

3. Stop attaching excess meaning in terms of being accepted or rejected by society. Break free by respecting others for who they are, and respect yourself for who you are setting out to become

4. Strive to succeed in your life, by the means of what you want.

We Are All Co-Creators of the Universe

As humans, we are all literally co-creators of this universe. The universe is free to wonder and whatever we create within **us** manifests to become a physical part of this world.

This has been proven by humans time and time again already. The world is constantly changing based on our decisions and actions as each year goes by. It seems like every other year technology is being upgraded.

Humans have been on the moon. Up to 2,500 satellites are orbiting the atmosphere utilized for viewing other planets, navigation and forecasting the weather before it happens. The majority of communication satellites orbit at the same speed of the earth's natural rotation, all due to our thoughts, feelings and actions.

You are one with the power of the universe, along with the growing possibility of what you can potentially create within it. You are one with the stars, the sun, the moon, all the animals, insects, nature and every human being on this planet.

Everything in this world changes and grows according to each of our own individual input. Everyday we are continually BUILDING THE EARTH!

You are able to create virtually **anything** you want out of life. So, really think about the unlimited possibilities we all share for a moment...

What do you want to contribute to our universe?

As the world continues to grow, you also grow with what being a co-creator of this universe naturally offers you.

Other people are contributing to our futures in one way or another in this very moment as you use your kettle or wait for the latest computer. This is because they have purposely or accidentally already reclaimed their co-creator status. And it's time for you to join in the fun and begin to open yourself up to the earth and contribute something amazing for the world to see.

You are alive and in harmony with the universe, draw from this earthly power naturally offered to you. Animals and plant life instinctively take it upon themselves to adapt to the earths natural growing energies. Embrace the earth by expanding your natural inner potential! And when you begin to use your own thoughts and actions together with the universe, you will unlock the unlimited power **you** were **already** born with.

Children are being born everyday as new co-creators connected to this world that move, think, feel and breathe.

You have this higher status; so, say it to yourself and reclaim this powerful gift "I am a co-creator of this universe" since you are and should use it to contribute to the greater good.

What matters though, is if you decide to take this opportunity upon yourself to employ it and show the universe what you **can really do**. LIFE IS WAITING FOR YOU TO SHOW UP! Where are you my friend? Your future success is waiting, your life and the continuous growth and potentiality to give to the universe is waiting for you to make a positive impact FOR your life.

SHOW US! And allow the universe to be on your side.

Exercise

(Read this once before you do it for the first time)

1. Close your eyes.

2. Float up, out of yourself, up to outer space

3. Look down at the world from this place and recognize your unlimited positive potential of being able to create anything you desire in the world

4. Float back down into yourself and connect to the world with love and passion.

In a nutshell

1. What humans are capable of is absolutely incredible, and we can see it everywhere. Your heart beats, you breathe and live, therefore you are a co-creator just like everybody else

2. You are now living with the potentiality and growth with the universe to create whatever you want

3. What do you want to create within yourself for the future? Allow it to resonate within your heart and let the moon, stars and sun naturally guide you towards success.

4. The universe offers you the power to succeed, so use this as a symbol for the success you are truly worthy of and begin creating the feelings, thoughts and behaviours to show up in life, *"my fellow destined co-creator of the our world"*

Modelling

Modelling is the act of replicating human excellence. And we have been modelling successful people for a long time now.

During childhood you have modelled your parents and close friends. You have picked up on these behaviours and thinking processes that are still useful in your life today.

You can model what is successful because particular humans have already accomplished what you want, which means you can re-create it **for** yourself. Whether it being to display charisma in financial situations, dealing with stress, fixing a car or mowing the lawn.

Modelling the person that already has the level of success you desire is a great way into achieving it for yourself.

This does not necessarily mean you would copy exactly what a person does. But rather you must apply the useful thoughts and behaviours other people use TO yourself, in the areas of life that **you** want to become more successful IN.

Take some time to list some successful people that **already** have what you want to achieve. They can be idols you know personally, people you see on TV or read about in books and magazines. This will give you guidance and inspiration towards obtaining success in those areas for yourself, not to mention using the internet for **instant** information.

Do you want to know how to make money faster and more easily? Learn how to prepare a new dish? To view stressful situations in a way that empowers you? Learn to become more motivated towards what you want to succeed in?

You can model on a physical level by taking on the behaviours successful people use, by asking them questions about their mental sequences; what did you do? How did you do that? Then what did you do after that?

E.g. "How did you learn to be so successful?" "Well I did…" "Then what did you do?" "I believe…"

By asking these questions the person you are modelling will tell you exactly what thoughts and decisions drive their actions, and everything that led up to it. You can then replicate these principles for yourself in a way that makes sense to you.

We all have reasons for why we do things; otherwise we wouldn't be doing them. Why did you brush your teeth this morning? Why DO you want a more fulfilling life? You can use the power of why to discover yourself and new concepts and ideas from others.

If you take other peoples reasons for why doing things their way is better than your old way; you already have come up with reasons for why this new way of thinking will personally drive **you** towards success.

Always ask yourself this very important question: What is the difference that makes the difference to be successful in this situation?

People have inspirational stories and solutions to problems to gain success because however they used to think - is not how they consciously think **now** - and however they continue to **be** successful lies even more useful information.

You can also model on a deeper level without ever having to talk to that person by becoming **curious** about their internal world for a moment. All you need to do is ponder on the difference between a surface behaviour and an unconscious state of mental thought process, by figuring out WHY these people do what they do. You can do this by reading biographies or keeping your eyes peeled for information that drives others to succeed.

Why means: Because of which...you will do something

I have many people I aspire to, some not even alive right now, and I have all their biographies too.

Exercise

(Read once before you try it for the first time)

1. Think of a person that has the talents and life success you would like to model; maybe a famous celebrity or entrepreneur.

2. Now, visualize yourself standing beside your idol, and copy the successful ideas, thoughts and behaviours to reconstruct your self image to slowly match theirs

3. Turn to look at the idol you have just modelled, and reach out to shake their hand, finally being equal in your endeavours

When modelling others, make sure you come from a place of curiosity rather than judgment and use as many of your senses as you can.

In a nutshell

1. Modelling is reproducing what already works, so you can learn and cultivate the patterns within you

2. Anything a human has already done means you can model their behaviours and thought processes to learn how to do it too, if not even better

3. Seek out and model the humans that already have achieved what you want by asking and researching how and why they do what they do

Looking Out For New Learning

People talk about how they achieve in life.

A friend of mine named Carol took me to a friend of hers because she needed to collect some clothes for a photo shoot. I didn't think anything of it and agreed to go along with her. We finally made it to her friend's house and I notice an old sewing machine to my right and a clothes rack with a few garments on it. After carol went to the bathroom; I and her friend (Denise) sparked up a conversation, I asked her if she made clothes.

This is what she said:

Yeah. I sew all types of clothes for people. Lingerie, Evening wear and day wear. I make quite a lot of money now but before it was very hard to get my garments out on the market.

Me: What happened?

I became frustrated but was not willing to give up, so I tried harder and my clothes started to get noticed.

Me: how did you do that?

I don't know, it was hard at first and then it just felt easy to market my clothes to help grow my business. People spread the word fast, it's kind of funny how once you don't have anything and then you do (Said with enthusiasm).

Me: Wow that's great, how did you learn to become so successful...?

When you listen to others stories, you automatically experience their story for yourself. You visualize and experience certain feelings as you follow along. Just as you're reading this right now, you are experiencing this book in your very own unique way. And other people experience this book in another way.

While I was listening to her little story I was also picking out certain key points that I could use in my own life. So I was literally considering and applying certain things to myself.

Let's try to break down this conversation and lay out some of the things that really stuck out for me:

She said: I tried harder and my clothes eventually became noticed...

To me; this felt like if you try hard enough, you can get the things you want.
She said: It was hard at first and then it just felt easy...

What at first is hard - begins to get easy.

She said: It's kind of funny how once you don't have anything and then you do.

When you put your mind to it, you can achieve anything.

Now, when most of us listen to people's stories we do generally agree with what they are saying, and most of it makes perfect sense to us; **But how to use this effectively?**

Go into student with inspiration mode to find out if there is any useful information that you can use in your own life and apply it to yourself.

I once told a relatively big guy that if he had absolutely no fear of anything he took upon himself in his life, no matter how hard or impossible the task that he just went for it head on; if he had no restrictions or blocks in his life...

How would he feel if people flocked around him because they thought to themselves "I want the freedom he's got, I need to find out why he's so successful and how he feels when he does it?"

When I asked him this a feeling of revelation came over his face. He said "wow, imagine if that happened..."

That was two months ago; He is now physically fit and his girlfriend adores him. He finally managed to lose the access weight he's been dying to get rid of; by applying the fact that anything can be possible within his life! He just went for it and reinforced this principle by working out everyday like a mad man!

After he achieved what he wanted he thought to himself "why go back to the old way, when I have found a new and better way?!"

He came up with all the reasons for why this made better sense to him and went with it, while refusing to never return to his old way of thinking - and came up with reasons to never go back.

These reasons where: "Because I'll get fat again, my sex life will be rubbish and my girlfriend will stop telling me I'm hot: I love it!"

You can open up to any new learning by asking yourself this question:

"If this were my own thought, how would I use this?"

Look out for new learning and link these new ideas to situations you would like to apply them in. So if someone says "Man, some things in life are just worth smiling about" and as you listen to them, you can think to yourself "mmm, what's worth smiling about in my own life". Then discover in what it's like view things differently.

Here's some for you to contemplate on right now:

"Forming habits are easy when you stay focused on the pleasures you are gaining from it".

"Opening yourself to possibility, widens your potential and creativity"

"Choosing on what positive feelings you can focus on, is a choice that is made"

"Moving impacts your life's future emotions"

"Accomplishing means going for it right NOW"

You can model and learn from all types of people in the world and everyone has there own unique way of expressing how they succeed. This is especially useful when you actively make this work in your life to gain something amazing. You would have EARNED it all, just by listening to what someone said

Imagine saying to someone during a conversation in the future: I achieved this £1million house all because someone said to me "where you live represents the level of comfort and happiness experienced in life; and this is what started my business!" You could have personally reasoned many combinations in a second as to why you had to make this a must for you.

People show and tell you how to succeed all the time!

The key rule to make yourself efficient at this is to have an open mind towards **real** possibility. Never judge people! Only become curious about their successful thinking through inspiration.

Be aware of learning's that generate success and reason them for yourself to turn them into your own ideas, thoughts, feelings and behaviours.

The formula

1. Ask aspiring questions to find out. E.g. "How do you do that?"

2. Go into 'student with inspiration mode' and consider if the learning is something beneficial. (Listen openly and intently)

3. If it is, how can you link this new learning to situations in your life? E.g. "If this were my own thought how would I use this?"

4. Come up with more reasons for why this inspires you to create even more success. E.g. "The way how I'm thinking about this is useful because..."

The Achievement Formula

These are the four steps that you can use to achieve literally **anything** you want in your life; whether it being to find a new job, become a more confident person or to find your perfect partner.

1. Know what you want

First of all get a clear understanding and an overall outcome in mind of what it is that you want.

When you are driving or walking somewhere you have an understanding and outcome of where you want to be; otherwise you wouldn't know where you are going.

You can't climb up a ladder if you don't know where or why you're walking up to the top. You must gain a clear outcome in mind **first** of what it is that you want to achieve.

You must also discover what gaining this achievement will allow you to feel as a result of achieving.

1. What do you want?

2. What will achieving this allow you to feel?

2. Take action

After you have a clear understanding of what it is that you want - the next step is to; **make the decision to take action**!

If you were to come up with a goal but didn't do anything about it, you will get nowhere!

It's the same notion of you knowing your destination but just sitting in the car gawping at the steering wheel instead of hitting the gas. It's like being a runner hearing the whistle blow, but staying mindlessly in the 'set' position.

A little and/or massive action will cause an effect and this principle is attached to everything you want in your life.

Know that taking daily actions at your own pace is fine as long as you're **doing something!**
Take any action that you see fit, whether if it's only a very small step or a massive leap into learning something new!

3. Be alert

After you have taken action; notice what results you are getting!

Keep your awareness open and recognize what responses and outcomes you are receiving from your actions.

Notice if you are moving closer to your goals or farther away. And above all, learn from what you get. Don't stop because what you tried once didn't work; but always look for alternative ideas through inspiration.

Learn from what you get whether positive or negative and direct in a way that serves you. You can learn to not make the same mistakes again and even if you do, you can be reminded to learn from these prior mistakes too. This means you have a sense of...**Flexibility**

A large stone cannot go through the tinniest hole but water is flexible enough to go anywhere and always adapts along the way. Become as flexible and as flowing as water and continue shaping yourself into the person you want to be.

IF YOU ALWAYS DO WHAT YOU'VE ALWAYS DONE, YOU'LL ALWAYS GET WHAT YOU'VE ALWAYS GOT!

IF WHAT YOU ARE DOING IS NOT WORKING DO SOMETHING ELSE!

You may ask; **"what if I get frustrated and can't do it?"**

First of all there is no such word as can't; there is only will you? Or wont you?

Second....

4. Use frustration!

Use frustration as a burst of energy to help you succeed even more.

Usually when people go through a frustrating time, it means they are really trying hard to gain what they want and this is a good thing.

Frustration occurs when we are overloaded and this is where we come up with our greatest breakthroughs, it means we are really trying hard to succeed.

Frustration represent you are doing well and coping through limits to become more - and learning once again from life's lessons! Continue to adapt and change yourself until you succeed.

When you become frustrated relax, get excited and be thankful for your continuous effort to grow in higher self esteem.

Welcome frustration with open arms, it proves you are growing and dealing with your adaptations in your very own unique way, to become the life success you have always wanted.

The formula

1. First of all, know what you want to achieve, and why achieving this goal will benefit you in the long term

2. Take some sort of action in the pursuit of this goal everyday without fail

3. Notice what results you are getting, and if you trip up and fall on your ass, get up again. Learn, change and adapt towards your success

Be flexible in your approach. Use frustration as a sign of growth and never give up until you reach the given end of your goals

After you have achieved - set yourself up for the next goal!

Adventurer - Explorer

The adventurer

The adventurer starts a journey with the only desire to experience something new and exciting. The adventurer is spontaneous and moves with inspiration towards longed for desires and goals and encounters new situations along the way.

Adventures are fun, because we set out to make them fun and the more we parade in this feeling, the more great things we encounter and learn along the way towards gaining a more fulfilling life.

An adventurer sees an opportunity and just goes for it. Making everything that happens along the way exciting, exhilarating and fulfilling no matter what happens.

The explorer

The explorer is someone who becomes curious about future goals and starts to explore what this **yet to be felt** rewarding experience is all about.

When you are an explorer you wonder on all the amazing future feelings and experiences that have not yet happened. And as that curiousness grows stronger, you begin to take action towards discovering how owning these new future feelings will benefit you.

Do you view yourself as an explorer or adventurer?

Do you view yourself as both?

Stories about searching for treasure are based on exploration as new adventures begin to take place.

Whichever you feel like you are, decide now to take on this wonderful new adventure of exploration into your own hands to actively accomplish your goals.

The treasure in life and everything you have ever dreamed of is ready for you to obtain, START your new life's fulfilling journey!

Anything is possible when you put your certainty and your faith in the directions that allow you to grow: Just as the explorer and adventurer has set out to do so.

Have a cause and a purpose for being alive and practice what you are truly worth! It's when you have a **purpose** and a **cause** to do something that you will be driven to success.
Use this as a reminder for why you have already made the decisions to move towards your goals as you DESERVE SO MUCH MORE!

Are you an explorer? Or are you an adventurer?

In a nutshell

1. An adventurer spontaneously sets out to experience something new and enhancing every second

2. The explorer knows what is wanted and explores in all directions to obtain what is desired

3. Are you an adventure or explorer? SET OUT TO INTERGRATE BOTH!

Faith and Certainty

Having faith and being certain that things will work out keeps us moving in the pursuit of achieving the things we want.

Certainty

Reasons and generalizations allow you to believe and be certain that you will no doubt gain what you want.

When someone feels certain about something they make a record, on all the tools and abilities they have; and this verifies them being able to get the job done like a round wheel.

A peaceful woman noticed a lump in her stomach and immediately thought it was cancer. She felt hesitant to call the doctors because she was uncertain to what her doctor might tell her. She slowly began to feel depressed, since she thought it was a terrible disease that developed due to her smoking habits.

Her husband was soon enough informed about what was going on and immediately rushed her to the doctors.

Although feeling scared, the woman realized that she had to find out the truth rather than living the rest of her life in fear. She got an ex-ray and blood test and patiently waited for her results. After a week she was called in and began to prepare for the worst. The doctor looked at her smiled and said "it's just a small lump of gristle, it's harmless".

She felt relieved and excited for her renewed long life ahead - as she can now live the rest of her life with **certainty**.

When someone is not certain they doubt and this doesn't help in anything!

Certainty helps us to move forward because we have reasons and proof for why we will undoubtedly gain what we need to consciously feel excited about for the near future.

What are the reasons you can personally come up with to be certain that you can always achieve what you want?

Think of the facts based on: you can move, talk, and hear, see, feel, taste, think, learn, discover, create, choose, decide, take action and associate right now!

These qualities you **already** had before you started reading this book is proof enough that you can be certain of achieving your goals. **Review these amazing powerful assets you already naturally possess as a human being!**

Make your dreams a reality and feel certain about what **you can** truly be capable of in your life RIGHT NOW!

Faith

Faith is a feeling of complete trust that your desires are meant to be and does not need any external proof or validation. It is an allegiance to a positive and personal cause that is consistently reliable in the pursuit of your endeavours.

Having faith is a natural emotion that allows you to experience a perfect guidance, almost as if something positive has been promised to you. Take a moment to relax in uninterrupted silence to quite your mind, and you will experience a deep inner sense of centeredness.

Have faith in yourself. You are, after all feeling what **you** feel, so why not have faith in what you do and decide as well.

Without even being aware of it, we use our faith in every moment of the day.

How could you drive a car with opposing traffic separating you by just a line painted in the middle of the road preventing someone from crashing into your car killing you instantly?

You have faith that people driving in the opposing direction won't accidentally or purposely swerve into your lane. If you didn't have faith, how could you ever trust driving on a road like that? The answer is, you TRUST and have FAITH in **life**!

We also gain faith in people when they do creditable actions for us. We notice they must think positively about us, and so we naturally build faith and trust in their capability to do us right. This is the same when you grow in faith to do right by yourself.

You must stay in line with making your personal dreams come true by having faith that you will always continue to do what is best for yourself.

Are you the type of person that could betray your own soul? I hope not! Because people that do end up not being able to create the life they truly deserve.

We as humans ALL have faith, because life has already prescribed us the opportunity to feel uplifted everyday. Grow to notice that all positive yearnings *are* meant to work out for your benefit.

In a nutshell

1. Be certain in your deservingness to succeed. Come up with facts and reasons for why you must stand strong with setting out to create the start of a new future

2. Faith is what keeps us stable; living life without worrying! Have faith in yourself that you can succeed in anything you put your heart to

3. Your future is always in your hands right now and this makes you a powerful creator of your own destiny

Your Higher Self

Everybody possesses a higher self.

Your higher self manifest the strongest learning's held by your unconscious. In other words, your higher self manifests strong patterns and sets out to make them a more or less permanent part of your life.

Your higher self has an infinite source of power and will manifest more or less anything that is strong enough within you. In other words, when something becomes really important to you, your higher self will pick up on it and will begin manifesting.

Your **individual** higher self is your own and is very beneficial to you, since you can use it to radiate positive energies into your life.

Just like when you continue to think about things that are exciting in life, the more exciting events and feelings begin to show up according to how much attention and focus it's given.

Using conscious focus in terms of desire, enthusiasm, excitement, visualization, sounds, feelings and behaviours is what begins the process of overriding doubts or fears that maybe interfering with your personal growth.

If you are a person that prays, you contact God through your very own personal higher self. Your higher self is the gateway to experiencing a growing and expanding love in your life. This loving manifestation is used to connect with God in your very own unique way.

This does not mean our higher selves are religious in any way since we manifest regardless. But praying is done through your higher self and is the gateway to this connection; this connection can only happen fully if the conscious and unconscious are fully connected with one another in a positive way. God is pure, loving, infinite, holy, forgiving and loyal. Some would refer to the higher self as 'God within' (as a means of manifesting with the higher self) and can lead to the gateway of experiencing an infinite loving connection with god. (If you haven't yet established this connection already)

To contact your higher self then, you must embrace in this faith towards your higher self's infinite love that will always manifest what you want. When you acknowledge, believe and project faith in this way, your higher self (Or god) will play a more active part in your life.

Project a loving, trustful and humble energy with your higher self. When this connection becomes strong enough, you will find yourself becoming more at peace.

Exercise

1. Notice yourself and everything around you: people, insects, nature, and project a loving energy towards everything in any way you possibly can

2. You will eventually feel a sense of being 'one' with everything and this will lead you into a personal contact with your higher self

Quite your mind

1. Find a place where there is nobody around and no noise to disturb you

2. Get comfortable by sitting up or lying down in complete silence

3. Quite your mind by releasing all thoughts and become aware of the tranquillity of what silence offers you. You can stay like this for as long as you like. This exercise also helps you to relieve stress

Exercise

1. Ask God in an undeserved and humble manner "Please co-operate with me and help me to resolve this situation in my life"

You can also ask God for inner resolve or ask for love and friendship during the days of your life.

In a nutshell

1. Your higher self manifests the strongest patterns held by your conscious and unconscious minds

2. Once the conscious and unconscious are in co-operation with one another the higher self will manifest anything positive you need to experience in your life

The Present

Whatever you do **now** in this moment highly affects your future. If all you decided to do today is take action consistently towards your goals; tomorrow you're going to feel even better because you have already started to make a positive impact in your daily life. And this is a great way to keep your motivation going in the right directions.

The present time is in the middle of your future and past: whatever you do right now, not only affects how you're going to remember your life, but also contributes to what your life is growing to become.

THE TIME TO PLAN THE REST OF YOUR LIFE IS NOW, NOT SEVEN YEARS FRROM NOW!

Now in this moment is where every ounce of your power is; and NOW is a fresh new opportunity to use this power to change your life.

Some people settle for less and come up with phoney excuses like "I don't know what to do, what if it doesn't work, what if I become a failure?"

Ask yourself this question: How would you feel if you didn't do a damn thing at all, lived the rest of your life feeling like 'crap' and then reached the end of everything feeling deep regret, all because you made the wrong decision by not taking action as of now??!!

The whole reason why you have made the decision to use these techniques is to reap the rewards during this process of growing in higher self esteem: Especially when you know you can do something about it right now!

YOU REALLY DO HAVE COMPLETE AND ABSOLUTE CONTROL OVER HOW YOU PERCIEVE AND CREATE YOUR EVERYDAY LIFE!

Think about the ultimate pain you will experience if you don't take action, and consider the many empowering moments of self achievement you'll miss out on as a result. Life is a wonderful journey my friend and there is so much opportunity out there for you it's a joke!

Make your dreams happen and do not settle for anything less than you can be EVER because you really don't have a reason to. PLEASE! If you won't do it for yourself, do it for your family and your friends or the future of mankind! DO IT NOW!

The future

The future is a place of wonder, the unknown and the unpredictable. If we don't have a vision of succeeding; and goals of what we want our lives to be like within a month from now, we won't have anything to be passionate about during the process of living up to our deepest desires.

I truly believe that humans are on this earth with the gift of being creative. We are created to create things; new businesses, new ideas, new feelings, discovering new ways to live, new thoughts or even just a new meal.

It's about discovering what you are truly capable of and using your actions everyday to create the feelings in life you truly deserve.

The more actions we take, the faster we **will** achieve our goals.

Think of your ultimate success goal to be a train station called "result". And your train is starting at a station called "the beginning". Depending on how much action and effort you put into your goals will measure how fast your train gets to the station "result". If you do nothing, your train will go nowhere and will probably become rusty and old.

DON'T LET THIS HAPPEN!

When you notice where you are in your life everyday, you'll be less likely to lose track of where you are going - "oil your wheels!"

How would you like to start feeling in a week's time? **Make** your expectations GROW to be high and use the start of these two weeks to move towards these expectations you have created with yourself. After all this is where brilliant ideas, emotions and accomplishments come from - WITHIN: You create positive ideas from within the inside and apply it to every area of your life!

Little action is ALWAYS better than nothing!

Expectedly focus on what you desire, in the mind set of whatever you contemplate on will undoubtedly manifest in the nearest possible way.

Whatever seeds you plant will grow when you continue to water them, and you expect them to grow don't you? Since you know this, it makes you want to water them even more so they can grow faster and more beautifully.

HOWEVER, try not to expect results straight away. When you plant a seed you don't return to it the next day screaming "Where's my plant!?" Some people expect results right away and tend to give up because things don't seem to be moving fast enough. DON'T LET THIS HAPPEN! (Weeds may pop up in your life that 'try' to prevent your plants from growing, but it's your job to plant new seeds and grow better plants that adapt to life's daily problems.) It's not until after a few days the plant begins to grow and in two weeks time, it is abundantly clear that manifestation is taking place and it is up to you to preserve it.

Your conscious, unconscious and higher self will always bring to you what you desire. Become one with your three selves to manifest together in a unity of power to better your life.

Take a few steps each day for 30 minutes to an hour to improve in the things you want to improve in. Do it at a pace that is right for you, as long as you make some sort of an impact that brings you closer to your achievements you have succeeded.

Practice all the time if you can. **Remember**, your impact is based on how much you contribute to your life.

Live your life a way that everything happens for a reason and purpose that serves you. Be certain that you are being led down a path in ever growing love, power, happiness, peace and success.

You deserve everything wonderful that is becoming a part of your daily life.

Stronger weaknesses exercise

1. Focus and bring up to the surface all the weaknesses you've had

2. Acknowledge to yourself that your weaknesses have made you stronger a still are

Say to yourself "My weaknesses make me stronger and give me power!"

Last Exercise

1a. Look into a mirror and playfully talk to yourself.

E.g. encourage yourself, compliment yourself, make yourself laugh, act silly, act confident and use just about any positive uplifting thought, behaviour and feeling you can think of in relation to your higher self esteem. Unleash your wonderful personality upon yourself with full engagement for as long as you like. Appreciate YOURSELF for how **good** you are making yourself feel.

1b. Imagine the you in the mirror is a real person that is now talking to you from an outside point of view

In other words, dissociate from yourself; almost as if everything the you in the mirror does, is expressed and directed at you.

Compliment and praise yourself, realize there is someone out there that cares about you, **YOU!**

Open up to yourself, accept and love everything you get to know about yourself and grow in self appreciation for who you are becoming.

My story

When I allowed my negative emotions to control my life, I lost everything! I was afraid of talking to people, I lost all my confidence, I was afraid to go outside, I felt like my family didn't support me, I lost all my friends, I thought people were always against everything I did, I became a drunk, a pot head, I lost all hope for the future and came to a point of wanting my life to end. I had **no one;** not even myself to count on. I blamed people, I blamed myself and even blamed god for why my life was completely soaked in ruin. I literally lost all hope living!

I began to hate the world and everyone in it. I started to adapt an evil attitude because I thought it was the only way to gain respect from others. I went out of my way to make others feel inferior. I even started to look up to people who subject in hate, revenge and violence. I went from being completely passive, to an attempt of being a self centred arrogant 'prick' of the world because I thought it would make me feel better.

However, I realized soon after that people hated me even more, to which only made me feel even worse. At the time I thought it sounded glamorous, but soon after I realized that the outcomes for my actions only lead to more pain, not only for my own future, but also for the way how I made other people feel around me.

I personally came to the conclusion that humans are naturally alive to care about each other. It should never be about what we've got or how first appearances lead us astray; But rather finding a special place inside of ourselves to care about others.

I really consider my outer skin as something that is not important what so ever, because when I adapted the notion of: It's not what I look like or how I dress or what I have, but rather how I feel within myself, what I am capable of for the future, my connections with others and how I can contribute to others lives is what enabled me to see the world and my life in a way that's right for me.

I believe god has given me a purpose. And who knew something so negative in life could turn out to be so wonderful in a way that allows us to grow, just by changing a direction of focus and action.

I will do my best to make sure that no one goes through the torment I have personally been through during my life at the age of 17!

How about you, what have you been through in your own life? - EVERYTHING happens for a **reason** that allows you to become more!

Encourage yourself now to discover your own purpose that relates in you being able to contribute love, peace, power, happiness and success in your own life and the lives of others around you.

Embrace everything in your life and remember; your manifestation is in direct reaction to your life's contribution. And I promise that you definitely will gain the wonderful rewards you actively create.

Exit

I want to take this time to let you know how much I respect you as a person. We are all human beings alike that are only different according to our past life experiences. We always wish we could've done things in a better way and we all make mistakes.

If you think about it, we are already connected since we share a thing called life: We breathe, our hearts beat, and we think and love one another all the same. And if this entire world where to connect with one another in a peaceful, happy, successful, respectful and loving way this world will become something so absolutely beautiful beyond any of our wildest dreams! (Well at least I think so anyway)

Hopefully this book has touched you on some level or another to discover this for yourself…

Look out for me in the future and in the mean time become abundant in the love you have for yourself and share love with other people in your life. I wish you all the very best in all the success, positive emotions, thoughts and behaviours that create the life experience you have always dreamed of.

*By the way: I'm **only** 20 years old (Born March 19th ^{1986} to be exact) and I have experienced inner turmoil and survived at the age of 17! And I started writing this book exactly a month after my 20th birthday. I built myself up all over again from the **very bottom** and managed to do well for myself. I'm guessing you're not starting from a low point like I was, so this should be easy for you, to begin changing your life for the better starting from today -*

RIGHT NOW. So let this be an example of what is TRULY and somewhat FREAKISHLY ***possible*** *for us all as LIVING breathing human beings.*

Thank you for this opportunity in allowing me to share with you.

Embrace everything in your life and expect that miracles will happen. God bless you!

To live is a gift

See you in the real world,

Nicholas Finnegan

www.ingramcontent.com/pod-product-compliance
Ingram Content Group UK Ltd.
Pitfield, Milton Keynes, MK11 3LW, UK
UKHW041946190726
13854UKWH00004B/1813

9 781425 114701